YOU'LL NEVER GET NO FOR AN ANSWER

Jack Carew

SIMON AND SCHUSTER

NEW YORK · LONDON · TORONTO · SYDNEY · TOKYO

*To my father John T. and mother Betty
whose indomitable spirits are everywhere
to be found in this book.*

Copyright © 1987 by John H. Carew, Jr.
All rights reserved
including the right of reproduction
in whole or in part in any form.
Published by Simon and Schuster
A Division of Simon & Schuster, Inc.
Simon & Schuster Building
Rockefeller Center
1230 Avenue of the Americas
New York, NY 10020
SIMON AND SCHUSTER and colophon are registered trademarks
of Simon & Schuster, Inc.
Designed by Eve Kirch
Manufactured in the United States of America

10 9 8 7 6 5 4 3 2 1

Library of Congress Cataloging in Publication Data

Carew, Jack.
    You'll never get no for an answer.
    1. Selling. I. Title.
HF5438.25.C33   1987   658.8′5   87-13043

ISBN 0-671-62495-4

Acknowledgments

The concepts and principles developed in this book have been many years in the making. So it seems only fair to thank those who first endured the high-sounding claims of the author and encouraged his progress toward publication—that is, his immediate family. Wife Barbara, daughter Patty, sons Sean and Kieran all contributed immeasurably to the earliest drafts of *You'll Never Get No for an Answer.*

For professional editing and publishing skills, I am indebted to many others—to Oscar Dystel, who first saw the publishing potential in this project; to my agent, Henry Morrison, who never takes "No" for an answer; to Michael Korda, editor-in-chief at Simon and Schuster, who influenced and shaped the book in many important ways; to Jack Romanos, president, Charles Hayward, publisher, and the outstanding sales and marketing team at Simon and Schuster who have dedicated much time and energy toward putting this book into the hands of people who can use it most.

For many patient hours of editorial guidance, I thank Edward Claflin of Brookside Press, who himself is an outstanding sales professional. He was unrelenting in his dedication. Ed labored with me every page of the way to produce this work for the sales profession—and for that I am very grateful.

In many respects, this book is a salute to the tremendous skill and loyalty of my two associates, Joe Cascarelli and Andy Sloan, who purchased the time for me to devote to this effort.

My thanks, also, to my son Sean, who helped to shape, move and stimulate ideas—and stood by my side during the darkest hours; to Harriett Graves, who followed the long journey through several drafts; and to Ursula Obst, whose notes, amendments and final touches brought the book to its present form.

A number of organizations and individuals were instrumental in shaping the attitudes and disciplines that guide Carew Positional Selling Systems. I would like to acknowledge the U.S. Marine Corps for teaching me the disciplines of organizational management and sound strategic planning; and the Mead Corporation, for providing me with a forum for growing people as well as a foundation of support for creative research and development.

By validating my research, scrutinizing programs, and bringing in fresh ideas, Dr. John E. Jones of Organizational Universe Systems breathed life into every element of training that we do today. Every participant in our programs has been influenced in profound ways by the impact of his planning.

My thanks to Ted Dimitriou, Chairman of the Board of Wallace Computer Services, my first and very valued client, who stepped forward and said: "Jack, I want the best sales professionals in the whole world. Make them for me." That was the original charter of my company—and it remains the challenge that we face today.

Above all, I want to acknowledge my debt of gratitude to the thousands of sales professionals who were my R & D, bringing me their pain, their stories, and their excitement. They are the heroes who, every day, quiet and unnoticed, bring dignity and pride to a magnificent endeavor, the profession of selling.

This is
A BROOKSIDE PRESS BOOK
published by Simon and Schuster

Contents

10 CONTENTS

To the Reader

For the many women who are now sales professionals or soon to enter the field, I want to make a special acknowledgment—and add a note about the language I have used in this book.

I am well aware that the sales profession has been dominated by men for many generations. As a result, women often face discrimination, indifference, and deliberate resistance at many levels of our profession. While some of the barriers are fading, others still exist—and I regret that the scope of this book is too general to address the specific issues raised by women in sales.

I am, however, confident that the standards of professionalism established through the use of the strategies in this book will strengthen the position of *any* salesperson, irrespective of sex or race.

While I have referred to "salesperson" and "customer" in nonsexist terms whenever possible, I have used male pronouns for the customer whenever a singular pronoun was required. For this I apologize, but I hope that female readers will be able to accept the pronoun as a sexist substitute for the nonsexist, but incredibly awkward, s/he.

1

This Book Is About You

I want to tell you how this book came into existence.

The seed was planted a number of years ago when I participated in a ceremony at a military academy honoring a friend who was killed while serving on active duty in the U.S. Marines. In his honor I presented to the academy a medal for valor and bravery that my friend had been awarded posthumously.

Following the formal ceremony, I was talking to the dean of students about the careers that graduates pursued once they had fulfilled their military contracts.

"What are their career choices if they don't stay in the military?" I asked.

"Jack," he replied, "we have two kinds of graduates in civilian careers. We have the professionals—that is, those who go into medicine, law, engineering, and teaching. Then we have those who fail to make it as professionals, and they wind up going into sales."

. . .

13

The dean's words came as a shock. At that time, I was a commissioned salesperson selling corrugated boxes (I *preferred* to call them "packaging systems") in the New York metropolitan area.

Until the dean said those words, I had never considered myself someone who had "failed to make it." I *had* thought of myself as a professional. My chosen profession was one in which I had considerable pride—and which was beginning to reward me with substantial income.

My profession had other rewards, too, that I might have enumerated for the dean. It gave me independence and a sense of achievement. It allowed me to associate with outstanding business people who were creative managers and high achievers. It tested my skills and abilities. To be good at my profession, I was discovering, I had to use *all* my resources.

But I didn't have an advanced degree in *selling*. And that certainly made a difference to the dean. As he made so clear to me, salespeople as a group suffer from a lack of professional acceptance and social respectability.

Are we salespeople—as the dean implied—just because we haven't succeeded in other professions? Is our selling just bootcamp preparation for management and more advanced responsibilities?

Recently I related the story of my encounter with the dean to the publisher of Simon and Schuster.

"Jack," he told me, "that story really hits home because I had a similar experience. I graduated from a small prep school where many of my classmates went on to become lawyers, doctors, and MBAs. And I had become a salesman—selling books.

"I'll never forget going back to my class reunion. When the headmaster asked me what I was doing these days, I mumbled something about being 'in publishing.' I couldn't bring myself to tell him I was a *salesman!* I just couldn't say the word."

The problem is *image.*

And it's a big problem—for us, on the receiving end, and for people in business who don't understand the value and importance of what salespeople do.

If you've read any books on the subject of selling—and what salesperson hasn't—I'm sure you're tired of being *told* you are a professional. You don't need someone to tell you so.

The fact is, ours is a demanding profession that requires stamina, courage, and discipline. If you have been selling for any length of time, you already have developed the tools of your trade:

* Human skills—to understand and relate to people as individuals
* Technical skills—to match your product or services to the customer's needs

Salespeople work in an intensely competitive arena, where they are being tested every day. Just consider:

You are never psychologically safe. You often face rejection and resistance to your ideas. Any customer can turn you down. A long-awaited order may be canceled.

You must conquer distractions and interruptions. Your task requires endurance. You have to persist until you get a commitment. *You* are the person who brings in the business. Your organization relies on your success to keep its doors open.

You have no place to hide. Your success and failures are out in the open for everyone to see. And pats on the back are few and far between when you fail.

These are stressful factors, but most successful salespeople handle them well. They have to. It goes with the territory, as we say in the trade. Selling requires the mental readiness to respond to stress and the emotional stamina to conquer self-doubt. Without any warning, you'll have to adjust to a wide range of emotional shifts, from the sheer exhilaration of closing a big sale to the devastating setback of an unexpected rejection. To handle these frustrations, you need to be persistent and resourceful—and you have to have bounce-back capability.

Whether you've been selling for twenty days or twenty years, you know that it takes more than contrived enthusiasm and memorized sales pitches to be successful.

During the time that I have been employing the strategies presented in this book, I have met many salespeople who have *all* the potential they need to be successful—but they lack the ability to execute.

What they (and you) have to do is chart your course to success on a steady and consistent basis by doing the right things at the right time with the right people.

For too many people, selling is like running a race with no finish line in sight. They do the same things day in and day out, with no concrete sales call objective and no plan for execution. They don't take the time to say, "Here's what I want to accomplish—and here's how I plan to do it."

More often than not, salespeople's skills and training are acquired *on the job.* We have very few academic opportunities in which to discuss sales strategies or compare operating procedures, or experiment with different modes of behavior to find out what impact our sales styles have on other people.

I've met salespeople in every industry who started out with virtually *no* professional education at all. It's as if they were expected to learn their profession by osmosis. Without being given methods for performance, they are expected to know instinctively what to do. The result is that selling becomes a seat-of-the-pants, feel-your-way-through-it set of activities for hopeful wishing and fancy guesswork.

Here are just a few examples of how people start out.

During his first week with an industrial supply company, a new rep gets a tour of the plant and several interviews with product managers. Toward the end of the week, he has a half-hour briefing with the head of his department. Then he's handed a route map and a computer printout of prospects. "Good luck!" says his boss, as he shakes the young man's hand and shows him out the door.

A woman doing public relations work for a Madison Avenue advertising firm is promoted to a sales position. During her long lunch with one of the principals of the company, she listens expectantly while he extols the great opportunities, talks about his own success, and pumps her up by telling her she can do it. "We think you'll represent us very well," he tells her. With that encouragement, her new job begins!

In a meeting room inside one of America's top office-product distributors, ten salespeople doodle on yellow lined pads while product specialists describe the features of equipment they'll soon be selling. After a day of this—and an inspirational film—the sales reps are reminded of their quotas and are instructed to "fix bayonets and take the hill!"

Believe it or not, in some sales settings these are fairly popular ways of getting people prepared for the profession of selling. Everywhere I go, I see salespeople on the job who are loaded up with technical information but totally unprepared to deal with the human side of selling. Through no fault of their own, they are starting off on the wrong foot. And the ones who *fall down least often* make it to the top!

In fact, my own experience was typical. My first sales job was with a prestigious manufacturer of cotton fabric in New York's garment district. For training, I was sent to the Philadelphia Institute of Textiles where I received *one day* of instruction. The rest of the time was spent learning about my product and then riding shotgun with experienced salesmen. I listened to the war stories of their successes and heard their beefs about the company. Following this, I was armed with forty pounds of samples, handed my hit list, and told to get orders.

Good luck, Jack Carew!

Married, with one child to support and another on the way, I was *desperate* to sell and make a living. I had no expense account, no company car, and my salary was so low that by the end of each month I had to borrow subway fare from the landlady just to get to work.

Today I meet salespeople in a variety of selling environments who find themselves in the same jam I was in back then. At the time in our careers when we most need guidance, support, and assistance, we are *least* likely to get training. We are told a lot about product—the nuts and bolts of what we are selling—but never given an education in how to understand what's important to the customer, position our solutions to his problems, handle resistance, and get a commitment to action.

For beginning salespeople, the manager's war stories may be entertaining, and the motivational films inspiring—but when the dust clears and your exuberant mood subsides, you have to face the reality of, "Do I—in a face-to-face engagement—know how to persuade the customer to buy from me?"

Veteran salespeople, I've found, have a different problem.

Many experienced salespeople lose their skills after a while because they are calling on established accounts where there isn't as much demand for flawless execution. They're already in the door, so a lot of their selling becomes dependent on a more social, personal touch rather than a precise, professional method.

This is how many salespeople lose their edge: They take the account for granted. They're not as mentally focused on the selling procedure because in many cases the system has been sold and they're simply maintaining the relationship.

The result:

BEGINNING SALESPEOPLE WILL TRY *ANYTHING* JUST TO *MAKE* A SALE.

VETERAN SALESPEOPLE WILL TRY *NOTHING* FOR FEAR OF *LOSING* A SALE.

The upshot is, many salespeople come to believe that methods and disciplines for selling are not necessary for success. Too many rely on "This-works-for-me!" formulas. They believe that working hard and getting the customer to like you is all it takes to make it. Their theories are actually little more than war stories. Their accomplishments are based on good luck rather than good practice.

If this has been your personal experience as a salesperson—if you were thrown into the job at the beginning and you feel as if you're swimming as fast as you can just to keep your head above water—then I hope this book will provide an island of refuge for you.

Here's a chance to drop out for a moment, to see where you've been and ask yourself about the skills you possess. This book may shed some light on things that have worked for you in the past. It will also provide you with the opportunity to look ahead and plan for your personal and financial future by revealing some strategies that can make the next stretch *significantly more rewarding* for you.

In this book, you will find that I don't hold up any multimillionaires as symbols of success. *Rich* salespeople are not the only *successful* salespeople. There are other things besides money that matter:

- Counting for something in the customer's eyes
- Being looked up to as an achiever by your colleagues
- Getting satisfaction from helping somebody out of a jam
- Getting a thrill out of helping your customers solve their problems and achieve their goals

It is important to measure your success in terms of your own values. Each of us takes away our own reward from the marvelous customer contacts that are the lifeblood of selling. It's these rewards that need to be put in the equation along with making a buck when you consider what you gain from your profession.

The truly great salespeople are those who practice their vocation at the highest level of competence and caring, and build careers on standards of excellence. These people help us all by bringing enormous credit to our chosen profession.

Selling is a series of day-to-day setbacks and personal triumphs. Every one of us is subject to very high peaks and extremely low valleys. We invest ourselves in what we are selling, and there is an emotional cost in doing so. We must be prepared to meet the extremes of satisfaction and disappointment that can occur within moments of each other, and still operate effectively in environments that test us constantly.

In this book you'll find that I discuss some of the conflicts and turmoil that we face every day. Rejection, anger, frustration, and disappointment are facts of life for salespeople. It won't help us to pretend that these feelings don't exist. It *will* help us to believe that we can deal with them.

That's what this book is all about—presenting you with clear, standard-setting methods of behavior that are now being employed successfully by thousands of sales professionals around the world. These strategies can be a powerful force for breaking the *cycle of frustration* that many salespeople experience in their daily lives.

But strategies are only as good as the mental and emotional chemistry that forms your attitude about yourself and the customer.

You may know *how to perform* adequately, but unless working for the customer's best interest is your underlying, primary purpose, you forfeit the total value you can bring to the selling profession.

The philosophy behind this book is simply this:

YOU WILL DO THE BEST FOR YOURSELF
WHEN YOU ARE DOING YOUR BEST
FOR SOMEBODY ELSE.

You will be able to say you have done your best at selling when you satisfy your customers' needs on a steady and consistent basis. As a professional salesperson, you can't *satisfy* those needs unless you know what they are and appreciate the person who has them.

For this reason, the strategies in this book focus on you and your *relationship* to your customers.

Are these strategies relevant to you in your sales arena?

To help you find out, I encourage you to ask yourself some questions about what you are doing now:

• Do you ever feel intimidated or unsure of yourself when calling on a top manager?
• Does your mind occasionally wander while the customer is giving you important information?
• Do you sometimes find yourself talking just to fill the silence?

- Does it take you four or five sales calls to accomplish what you might have done in one or two?
- Do your established customer relationships seem boring?
- Have you ever lost an order because someone you never met influenced the buying decision and turned it against you?
- Do you get more kick out of off-the-job activities—such as sports, politics, and hobbies—than you do from selling?
- Do you find making an initial sales call more difficult than making a sales presentation with an established account?
- Do you become impatient listening to a customer talk on at length when you already feel as if you have a solution to his problem?
- Do you ever have a day when you run out of energy for no apparent reason?

If your answer to a majority of these questions is "yes," then I believe you will find great value in the strategies that are outlined in this book. These are just some of the many questions that will be addressed.

These strategies are more than theory. They are action planning. Each applies to a very specific aspect of your relationship with the customer. Among these strategies are methods for:

- Building the customer's trust and confidence
- Turning resistance into acceptance
- Determining what's important to the customer and matching your ability to respond
- Making effective presentations and earning a commitment to action
- Building the relationship and expanding its possibilities
- Satisfying the customer's needs, with a pay-off to you and your company

To help you achieve these objectives, I will help you *visualize* what you *do*.

As an integral part of this book, we are going to combine selling attitudes and actions into visual models. These models will form a memorable framework for every sales call.

These are models that I developed some time ago for myself. Because I have a strong visual orientation, I felt that sketched out diagrams were necessary in order to remind me of where I was going during sales calls. By creating these diagrams—or *process models,* as I call them now—I was able to see at a glance what key things I was accomplishing at any given time. The models were a kind of road map to help me *see* what I was *saying.*

When I showed these models to other salespeople and described their processes, I soon discovered that the *visuals* helped communicate what I was trying to say about a number of my strategies. And today, the process models for building a relationship, determining customer needs, and making a presentation carry *instant meaning* to people who actively employ these strategies. (Incidentally, that includes non–English-speaking salespeople. The graphic models have proven helpful around the world, transcending language barriers among sales professionals!)

These models are not complicated. I don't want them to be. I have intentionally made them as clean and crisp as possible so that they deliver a simple message—reminding you where you are, where you are going, and what you want to achieve on any given sales call.

Once you embrace the *philosophy* of this book, master the *strategies,* and learn the *models,* the result will be that you are *in position* as a salesperson. This is why I call my method "Positional Selling," and the tools for its implementation the "Ten Strategies for Positioning."

For marketing and advertising people, *positioning* is an overriding concern: "Do we position this brand as a luxury item?"

"How do we position this product with consumers?" "How will this sales campaign change our position in the marketplace?"

Salespeople need the same awareness of positioning. You are marketing *yourself* as well as your product or service. *You* are the creator of your own position.

Positioning is forging favored status with the customer. Your very presence in the relationship becomes the reason for buying. You become the standard by which all other competing products and services are judged.

All things being equal, *you* make the difference.

When you are *in position,* you have favored placement in the customer's decision-making process. The customer will know:

> "There's nothing really different about what Mary's selling except Mary—and I'm *betting on Mary* to make this work for me."

In describing and illustrating for you the Ten Strategies for Positioning, I am mindful of the fact that there are thousands of different selling arenas. My own experience certainly doesn't encompass all of them. But I do know that the Strategies for Positioning have universal application. *Every* salesperson can use them, no matter what he or she is selling.

Positional Selling strategies have been used by a wide range of organizations selling an enormous number of different kinds of products and services.

Positional Selling strategies work in the stern confines of a corporate boardroom while selling a complicated financial planning system; or while selling insurance in the comfortable surroundings of a potential customer's living room.

They work in the antiseptic atmosphere of a medical testing laboratory as well as on the muddy construction site as you're selling potential buyers their dream home.

These strategies work in the rushed and congested atmosphere of an industry trade show as well as the plush setting of a corner office.

They work on Fortune 500 industry leaders as well as on medium-to-small-size backbone industries of this country.

Positional Selling strategies work anywhere, anytime, and with anyone.

Positional Selling is a way to sell *anything people need*—and that includes automobiles, life insurance, investments, capital equipment, industrial products, books, philanthropic causes, advertising, education, food, clothing, entertainment, just to name a few.

The concepts and principles of Positional Selling cross cultural lines. The strategies of Positional Selling are achieving phenomenal results in a host of different cultural environments including South America, the United Kingdom, and throughout Western Europe and the Middle East. They work in the very formal and stern Swiss business environment as well as the carnival atmosphere of Rio de Janeiro.

Positional Selling strategies are as applicable to a Lebanese sales professional selling to a Saudi purchasing officer as they are to a Swedish systems engineer selling to an Italian data processing manager.

I emphasize the *universality* of the program not to tout the power of Positional Selling but to make a more important point:

POSITIONAL SELLING IS NOT ABOUT *WHAT YOU SELL.*
IT'S ABOUT *YOU, THE SALESPERSON.*

How you organize yourself and your business, how you prepare for a sales call, and how you respond to the demands placed upon you by your customers or clients—these *strategic decisions* about your own positioning have more impact on your career than the particular product or service you are selling today.

When an MBA acquires management skills, he or she is prepared to apply those skills in *any* organization within *any* industry. When you acquire the selling skills described in the Ten Strategies for Positioning, you are *preparing* yourself to apply those skills in any field of public or private endeavor.

I can't think of a time in history when salespeople have been more important. Every day, every one of us is making a serious contribution to our economic and social communities. The *quality* of that contribution is shaped by our behavior, our industriousness, and our inventiveness.

After listening to and working with many salespeople, I have begun to observe that this decade has introduced a sweeping change of mood. The message of the Seventies was *"Me, me, me."* The themes of this time were expressed in books such as *Looking Out for #1,* songs like "I've Got to Be Me," and phrases such as "Doin' your own thing." There was a preoccupation with "What's in it for me" that, in effect, denied that we are interrelated human beings, that we all need each other in order to succeed.

In the Eighties, it seems to me, there is a growing concern with looking out for the other person. Songs like "We Are the World" and events like "Hands Across America" indicate a reawakened consciousness of our responsibility to others. And salespeople are a vital part of that changing mood.

Positional Selling is a strategy for the Eighties and beyond. It sets the other person's interests above your own. It gives you strategies for communicating, caring, and responding.

With Positional Selling you have an opportunity to breathe new life into account relationships—and open the door to fresh opportunities. You do not have to play a guessing game on every sales call. Positional Selling gives you the strategies for winning in such a way that other people win along with you.

·   ·   ·

I must admit that I bring a *practical* bias to this book. I am talking from the inside—not the outside—of the sales profession. Positional Selling strategies are based upon experience. They have been tested and proven in the most demanding sales environments—and they work. There have been times when I turned away in despair and defeat. I know what it's like to feel self-doubt and to vacillate between anguish and rage. And at one time in my life I paid a high price for having no skills, no direction, no plan, and no long-term goals.

But the strategies of Positional Selling changed my life as a salesperson. I discovered that I did not have to rely on a hit-or-miss approach to selling.

With the Ten Strategies for Positioning, you *overcome* self-defeating attitudes and *eliminate* guesswork. The difference this makes in your performance is significant. When you implement the Strategies of Positional Selling, you set standards that are so high, all your competitors must be judged in comparison. You occupy favored placement in the minds of your customers because you are doing the right things *before, during,* and *after* every sales call. When your customers compare you to your competition, the decision can only go one way: *your* way.

That's why you'll never get no for an answer!

2

You Make the Difference

Now for a question.

Have you ever found yourself cooling your heels on a prayer bench in a drafty lobby next to a fake potted palm with gum wrappers and cigarette butts among the woodchips . . . and alongside you are half-a-dozen other salespeople waiting their turn and trying to stay awake while they thumb through tattered back issues of the trade magazines . . . and when the buyer finally comes out of his office and says, "Who's next?," you jump to your feet only to hear him tell you he's only got a minute and to make it quick because he's got a lot of people to see today?

Does that sound familiar?

I'm sure it does. Because you and I and every other salesperson have been in situations *just as bad as this* many times before.

Now, let me ask you another question.

How do you *feel* in that situation?

Would *powerless* be the right word?

Helpless?

Out of position?

Well, let me assure you that feelings of powerlessness and helplessness are not confined to dingy gray waiting rooms in industrial office buildings. You don't have to experience the discomfort of a torn-up vinyl chair next to a fake palm tree to feel that you are out of position.

You can feel just as powerless sitting in the boardroom of a Fortune 500 company waiting for the chief operating officer to appear. You can feel helpless behind the best table in a five-star restaurant with an eighty-dollar bottle of wine on the table and a waiter in a penguin suit at your beck and call. You can feel out of position in the middle of a crowded floor during a trade show, waiting behind your own desk for an unhappy client to appear, or riding the elevator up to the thirty-second floor to see a buyer who's waiting to eat you alive.

In fact, a lot of salespeople feel that way *all the time.*

How do I know? Because I've felt that way myself.

And I had to discover, for myself, that there are things you can do to *change those feelings.*

There are things you can say—and ways you can act—to take feelings of powerlessness and convert them into opportunities for status in the sales relationship.

But before you can make that change, you have to *want* to make that change.

That was a lesson that didn't come easily.

Even in my days as a freshman salesman, I faced some major-league buyers. I knew buyers who would eat ground glass for dinner. They chewed up salespeople and spit them out just for the fun of it.

Selling yard goods in the garment district of New York was my first job after leaving the Marine Corps, where I'd been a platoon commander. Now, in the Marine Corps, I'd been through basic training and served in the South Pacific, and I'd been through many tests of endurance. But nothing in the Marines prepared me for what I was going to face on Seventh Avenue in New York.

My first boss was a guy named Harry ("the Horse") Goldman—*Mr.* Goldman, to those who worked for him. (To this day, I have trouble saying "Harry.") Now, Mr. Goldman was no tooth fairy, but he was tough and fair, and he taught me a lot about selling.

After a year on the job, he made me show him the entire line, which was low-end cotton fabrics sold to women's dress and sportswear manufacturers. I had to stand up and give a presentation just as if he were the piece-goods buyer, while he asked me a lot of questions and threw me objections designed to rattle my concentration.

I put on a great demonstration. I showed him the whole line as if they were the greatest bolts of cloth since God created Earth. I told him about the superior quality and, of course, I advertised the price—this is only 49½ cents a yard, and this is 69½ cents a yard. What a bargain! What a deal!

When I was all done, Mr. Goldman didn't look pleased.

"Young man," he barked at me, "*Forget the price!* You've got to *romance* the buyer!"

I said, "What do you mean, Mr. Goldman? We've got good prices."

"I know we've got good prices. But they won't buy from you because they love your price. They'll buy from you because they love what you're selling. I'm telling you for your own good, *romance the buyer!*"

Another thing I learned from Mr. Goldman was the difference between a *conversation of good intent* and a *conversation of commitment.*

One day shortly after I started, Mr. Goldman called me into his office.

"Well, young man," he asked, "how'd you do today?"

I'd been going since dawn, I hadn't made a sale, and I was exhausted. But I tried to sound enthusiastic.

"Very well, Mr. Goldman. I had a very good day."

"Did you get any orders?"

"No, but I met a great friend of yours, Lenny Bloomfield. He says he remembers you and your brother from temple and to send his regards."

Mr. Goldman looked at me. "Young man," he said, "I'm very glad Lenny Bloomfield sends his regards. *But did he give you an order?*"

"Well, no, Mr. Goldman, but we had a great conversation."

"I'm glad to hear that, young man," said Mr. Goldman. "But *unfortunately* I can't feed conversation through the computer in my order-entry department on the seventh floor. In the future, don't bring me conversation, bring me orders!"

He didn't need to say anymore.

The lesson took.

In fact, it took so well that I was able to apply that lesson—in the best way possible. About seven months later, I had worked my way up to become a leading producer on the sales force. This accomplishment was achieved by dint of steady, hard work. I'd been a long-distance runner in college, and that gave me a lot of stamina. I carried two forty-pound sample bags everywhere I went—I had the back of a weight lifter—and I worked from dawn to dusk. People gave me a chance because they saw I was trying. And once I got in the door, they could usually find something they wanted to buy from me. God knows, I gave them enough choices.

And my accomplishments were about to be recognized. As

I was on my way back to my desk one day, Mr. Goldman stopped me and said, "Young man, you are doing a very good job and I want to compliment you."

"I appreciate what you say, Mr. Goldman," I replied.

"I mean it. You're doing a good job," he repeated.

"That's really great, Mr. Goldman," I continued as I reached in my pocket and pulled out my wallet. "Unfortunately, Mr. Goldman, compliments don't put money in my wallet and they don't put bread on the table so I can feed my family."

He gave me a funny look. Then he laughed, shook his head, and went into his office and closed the door.

After a while the door opened and he stuck his head out.

"Carew, get in here."

I went into his office.

"I'm giving you a seven hundred dollar raise, effective immediately."

I later found out that was one of the largest raises he'd ever given to any beginning salesperson in the company.

To me, in those days, it was a fortune. It moved me up to the poverty level. Now I wouldn't have to borrow bus and subway fare from the landlady in order to get to work.

Life on Seventh Avenue taught me another thing: the meaning of emotional stamina.

It was a real eye-opener for me, fresh out of the Marines, to discover that I had to come to grips with feelings of impatience, frustration, and rage, and not strike back.

The first time I got chewed out by a customer, it nearly destroyed me.

I had called on a piece-goods buyer who said he wanted to make a purchase, but when I got there, we just couldn't agree on price. He wouldn't buy at the price I was giving him, and I couldn't go down even a half-cent a yard.

As we parleyed back and forth, I could see the buyer was

getting more and more impatient. Finally he turned to me and yelled, "You're through, you son-of-a-bitch. Get your ass out of here!"

I went into a state of high-level trauma. Except for boot camp in the Marine Corps, I'd never been spoken to that way.

"You can't speak that way to me!" I yelled back, clenching my fists. "I was a commander in the Marine Corps!"

He laughed in my face. "So? Big deal! Now, get the hell out of here!"

I got out of there, but the tears were welling up in my eyes as I went down six flights of stairs to the street. On the way back to the office, I stopped in the local church on 36th Street, got down on my knees and prayed for divine intervention.

No one showed up to help me.

Back at the office, I told the assistant sales manager about the incident.

"So what's the problem, Carew?" he asked. "Go back and tell the guy you're sorry."

"Tell him I'm sorry? But Morty," I pleaded, "the guy called me a son-of-a-bitch!"

"Look, Carew, do you want to be a salesman or not? You'd better decide now, because if you do, you'd better have *guts.* And if you've got *guts,* you'll go back and tell that guy you're sorry."

"Morty—I can't! I just can't *do* it!"

But in the end, of course, I did. After one more stop at the church on 36th Street, I returned to the buyer's office.

While I was in his waiting room cooling my heels, I tried to figure out what I was going to say and not lose face. Suddenly the buyer came bursting into the room. He took one look at my forlorn expression and burst out laughing.

"What's the matter, kid? Can't you take a joke? Now get your ass back in here and sell me something!"

About then, the real truth dawned on me: On Seventh Avenue in New York, *son-of-a-bitch* isn't an insult. It's a term of endearment!

The garment district was the first stage in the transformation of Lieutenant Jack Carew from Marine Corps Platoon Commander to a savvy, streetwise salesman. And I did get a little better, but it was mainly because people identified me as a hard-working, likable kind of guy who would bust his onions to do a great job. After a while I tasted some success and I started to make a few bucks. *But I was still a long way from becoming a professional salesperson.*

Then I changed jobs—and learned a few more valuable lessons.

My second job was with the Container Corporation of America, located in New Jersey, which manufactured and sold corrugated boxes. The pay was better, plus they gave me a new title—packaging engineer. For the first time in my life I had an expense account . . . and a company car!

My first day on the job was memorable.

My manager, Joe Horvath, took me down to the plant floor where there were about two hundred men and women working on the machines.

"Jack," he said, "now that you've come to work for us, there's something I want you to keep in mind. Do you see all of those people running those machines?"

I nodded.

"Well, I want you to think of them and their families when you're out there selling. Because if you don't do your job, I'm going to have to send them home."

That didn't exactly make me feel complacent in my new job. But it did make an indelible impression on me. I didn't forget Horvath's words—I didn't forget those people on the shop floor—and I haven't to this day. When I was out there selling, it was always at the back of my mind that I was selling for *them*.

That's the thing about being a salesperson:

YOU'RE THE PERSON WHO KEEPS EVERYONE ELSE EMPLOYED.

But the truth was, even though I now had some frontline experience, *I still didn't understand all there was to know about selling.*

Here I was, a marginally successful salesman, and I really didn't have an organized plan or method. I had no real idea what I was doing right and what I was doing wrong. I just knew I was doing something. It was hit or miss.

Most of my initial sales calls were random in nature. I never really had a solid, workable approach to initiating the transaction. If I were to summarize these calls, I'd have to describe them as "spraying and praying." I would lunge into the buyer's office and overpower him with a capability presentation (if you could call it that) without ever really finding out what he was all about and what he felt was important when he considered my product.

I was winging it.

Apart from not being able to make benefit statements, handle objections, and ask for the order, I was an outstanding salesman.

Fortunately the position I walked into on my second job protected me from having to make new-account sales calls. For the first year, nearly all my sales activity consisted of doing maintenance work in established accounts. These buyers didn't need to be resold, because they were already hooked on the company I worked for. My job was to go in and *protect* the coveted position a long line of predecessors had so energetically *earned.*

As it turned out, this kind of selling was a piece of cake for me. I lived up to everyone's expectations by diligently monitoring those accounts. I called on them every day of the week, with at least one significant social contact each weekend.

A lot of times I was given the business *just because I showed up.* I used to call on a company called Guardian Better Pack in the middle of the Bedford-Stuyvesant section of Brooklyn. It was the toughest neighborhood I've ever seen. The gutters were lined with dead dogs, cats, pigeons, and rats. I had to pay street kids a buck to watch the car while I went inside—otherwise, the car would disappear by the time I came out again.

That neighborhood reminded me of the impact zone of an artillery firing range.

The buyer, a man named Ben Krebs, was the same guy who ran the company. He respected me because I worked hard, and he gave me a lot of business because I had the guts to penetrate the killing zone.

One day he asked me why I worked so hard, and I told him it was because I wanted my kids to have new shoes and I couldn't afford them unless he gave me an order.

And I reinforced that statement by showing him a family picture.

After that, "new shoes" was the rallying cry.

Whenever I showed up, Krebs would say, "It's shoe-time! Carew's here!"

Then he'd order a truckload of boxes. "Here's for the kids' new shoes," he'd say as he handed over the order.

ALL I HAD TO DO WAS SHOW UP.

There was only one hitch to selling brown boxes.

I had to be willing to do just about anything for my customers.

It got to the point where I was more of a social director and tour guide than a salesman. One of my clients came to expect that I would always show up on Friday to take his wife, also the bookkeeper of the company, out shopping. (As it turned out, that paid off, because she would always defend me whenever there was a quality or late-delivery problem.)

I was called upon to emcee Christmas parties. I had to show up at bar mitzvahs, birthdays, and christenings. I delivered cut-rate liquor. I obtained airline tickets on fully booked flights, painted customers' houses, helped plant trees, and in general became so close to my customers that they would feel immoral if they betrayed me by giving their business to someone else.

On March 17, I always invited my customers out to the St. Patrick's Day parade in Huntington, Long Island, where I marched with my wife and three kids—all dressed in green hats, carrying shillelaghs. After they had braved the cold winds of March, I'd invite all my clients who showed up to come over to the house for corned beef and cabbage.

Sporting events were my forte. I had an inside contact at Shea Stadium. Name the game, and I could get seats. And only the best.

My sporting contacts were so extensive and influential that I was able to trade off tickets with other salesmen, giving me a wide range of choices for clients who had different preferences. They only had to tell me the event they wanted to see and where they wanted to sit and I'd get them in! Front row center, 50-yard line, center court, whatever. It made no difference.

I was more like a courier shagging tickets for sporting events than a salesman selling corrugated boxes. It got so bad that my customers began to expect me to deliver the impossible. I'll never forget the time I got tickets to a Beatles concert for the wife of one of my customer's friends—and she raised holy hell when she found out her seat wasn't right next to the stage. She finally agreed to accept a seat next to Brian Epstein, the Beatles' late manager.

And never thanked me.

I knew things had gotten out of hand when I found myself having to come up with tickets for my customer's brother's father-in-law who wanted to take his daughter's son to a Dodgers/Mets game as a reward for getting straight A's on his report card.

Now, I didn't perform all these recreational tasks out of a purely altruistic need to make people's lives more eventful and fulfilling. I did these favors because I wanted my customers to feel they needed my services in a variety of ways and, as a result, owed me.

I did these favors to obligate the buyer. And I would do anything. I didn't want my customers to dare entertain a competitive proposal for fear they would lose their best social activities go-fer.

My problem was that I was so busy manipulating people through personal favors that I failed to build relationships on professional performance.

Looking back on it, I now see that I was a psychological misfit. I had such a hunger for approval that I would do *anything* to avoid putting the buyer in a position where he could say "no" to me.

It paid off—I held on to a lot of business while asking for very few orders. But despite this, I was still not fit for the job of selling.

There were additional signs that something was wrong. I began looking to my *customers* for the emotional support I should have been getting from the home office. I needed a home base where I was psychologically safe; and already established accounts fit the bill just fine for a professional visitor like me.

After all, my customers were my friends. Whenever my company tried to put through a price increase, I would fight like hell to stop it. I wasn't interested in knowing why the increase was necessary from the company's point of view. All I wanted was to make my customers happy because they were the ones who were handing out the strokes.

Essentially, *I forgot who was signing my paycheck and I co-signed every ounce of my loyalty to the customers.*

There were many signs that something was wrong with my career—and if I'd been paying any attention, I would have noticed earlier. Outside activities were consuming more and more of my time—being at the top of my class in graduate school, getting promoted in the Marines, and reducing my golf handicap. Invariably, when salespeople aren't getting their needs met *on* the job, they'll begin to look for satisfactions *off* the job.

That's the way I was. I became more interested in succeeding off the job than on the job. I was getting *financial compensation* on the job, but I wasn't getting a *psychological paycheck* because no one was taking me seriously as a sales professional.

Least of all, myself.

And there was one other thing. I couldn't handle rejection. God forbid that I should leave the warm womb of established accounts and prospect for new business. Cold calling was not a nurturing experience, and it was psychologically draining for me because I didn't know how to deal with it.

In fact, to avoid real contact with new prospects, I found myself haphazardly driving off into Suffolk County or as far away as Connecticut, with no firm appointments, hoping that when I showed up, the buyer would see me. I rationalized these activities as "business development." But they were really *run and hide.* I would waste whole days on these highly speculative junkets hoping that I would get lucky.

I never did.

Because I had no goal.

I was just running around the sales track with no finish line in sight.

Slowly it dawned on me that if I was going to get better as a salesperson, I had to free myself from my dependency on putting people on the third base line at Shea Stadium on Sandy Koufax Day or painting their houses on weekends when I should have been with my wife and kids.

But how?

I vividly remember the turning point—because it was a significant moment for me.

It occurred one day when I was visiting a buyer named Eddie Call at Y & S Licorice near the Brooklyn Navy Yard. As I was waiting for him in the lobby, I happened to pick up a trade magazine—and a very interesting item caught my eye. It was the headline of a product advertisement:

"THE VALUE BUILT INTO OUR PRODUCT IS A MORE IMPORTANT ASSET THAN A LOWER PRICE."

That thought stuck with me. What if I used a phrase like that with the buyer? Could I make him *see* that the value of myself and my company exceeded any price consideration? Or would he laugh me out of the office for making such a wild claim?

It didn't take long to find out. A few minutes later I found myself in Eddie Call's office listening to him tell me that my prices were too high.

I took a deep breath and said, "Eddie, I can understand that price is an important consideration. But I promise you that the

value built into my offering and the commitment I will bring
to the relationship are more important assets than boxes you
could purchase from someone else for less money."

This seasoned buyer took a good long look at me and I was
certain he was going to tell me where to go. But when he finally
spoke, the words that came out of his mouth were: "Jack, you
have a very good point there."

And by the time I walked out of Eddie Call's office, I had an
order for one whole carload of boxes.

At the time, this was a very important breakthrough for me.
Up till then, all my sales calls had been like hitting golfballs in
the fog: I had a good go at it, but I was never really sure where
my shots would land.

All the things that are second nature to me now were completely foreign to me back then. I had never checked out a buyer
to find out whether I had a chance to get his business. I never
really attempted to find out what else it would take, *besides*
competitive pricing, to earn the right to a relationship. Like so
many salespeople, I had fallen into the trap of *mistaking activity
for accomplishment.*

And here, for the first time, I'd discovered a very simple truth
that was to affect the entire course of my sales career:

IF YOU SAY THE RIGHT THING AT THE RIGHT TIME,
YOU CAN TURN A TRANSACTION AROUND
AND SWING THE ORDER-GIVING DECISION IN YOUR
FAVOR.

This observation was reinforced a short time later in my
career, when I had the occasion to work with Fred Renshaw,
the corporate vice president of sales for the Alton Box Company.

Fortunately for me, Renshaw took an interest in my progress. One day he came to me and said, "Jack, you're a fine

young man. You're enthusiastic, you're dedicated, you're ready to set the world on fire. *But you just don't know how to sell!*"

That was a shocker. I was completely unprepared for a remark like that.

The good part was that Fred Renshaw would never cut you down without building you up again. So naturally I asked him what I could do to learn how to sell.

He said, "Let me show you how to *plan ahead* for an effective sales call."

That was a new one on me. I'd never *considered* planning a sales call. In the past, all my sales calls had been like spaghetti on a plate, running every which way. The idea of sorting out my ideas and making a coherent presentation was unimaginable.

But when Fred showed me how it was done, I quickly discovered there was a method for success, and a well-prepared sales call, supported with a written proposal, would make the customer pay attention and take me seriously.

Furthermore, a prepared sales call produced results. At that time, we were going after a very big account, American Cyanamid. By planning my presentation and supporting it with a written proposal, I not only cracked the account—*I got an order worth a quarter of a million dollars!*

That lit my fire. It had taken awhile, but I was finally beginning to realize that selling meant something more than being a great guy all the time. I had to engage in well-thought-out, professionally executed sales behavior instead of "winging it" as I had done in the past. There was a discipline here that I had never really explored and studied seriously. I could learn that discipline.

As I began to apply what I'd learned, I found that I was beginning to score where I'd failed in the past. I saw how the science and discipline of selling could work for me. And I realized that here was something I could pass along to other salespeople.

The selling skills that turned my career around *could work for every salesperson in the world!*

After that, I had a mission—to elevate my chosen field to the status of a profession.

Selling is a profession to be proud of. As Joe Horvath at Container Corporation of America reminded me, if salespeople don't do their job, everyone will have to go home for the very simple reason that there won't be anything for them to do.

Selling is a profession that *can* be learned. It's both an art and a science. It's an art because you bring to it the style and personality that distinguish you from any other person. It's all those things unique to you—your outlook on life, your values, your feelings, and your way with people.

Selling is also a science because it requires the conscious application of product knowledge and customer-sensitive communications skills. It can be said that in its most profound sense, selling is applied behavioral science.

There's another thing I've observed about selling.

It has to happen at different levels. At the *functional level,* you're saying, "I want to help you solve your problems." At the *interpersonal level,* you're building a relationship and getting the person to like you and want to do business with you. You're saying, "I want to solve your problems and build a lasting relationship."

If you confine your selling strictly to the functional level, you're selling from the neck up. You're using your head but not your heart. If you're selling at the interpersonal level, you're selling from the neck down. Heart, but no head.

Positional Selling is blending the functional and interpersonal sides of selling. You combine your sensitivity to the customer as a person with your commitment to being a problem-solver.

Which means:

YOU'RE ABLE TO ESTABLISH POSITION.

Being proud of what you're selling means *being proud of yourself.* You're always selling two products—yourself *and* your solution.

THE CUSTOMER WILL FIND SOMETHING WRONG
WITH WHAT YOU'RE SELLING
WHEN HE FINDS SOMETHING WRONG WITH YOU.

Conversely, the value that's added to any product is the value that *you* bring to the relationship. You always have to be willing to operate in the customer's best interest.

That could mean that you have to fight hard within your organization to make sure your company does the best it can for him.

It also might mean that you will have to work diligently to help him run his business more profitably.

Or it could mean that you have to step up to the line for him in his own organization and make him look good in the eyes of his associates.

It all comes down to this:

ALL THINGS BEING EQUAL
—PRICE, SERVICE, QUALITY, AND DELIVERY—
YOU MAKE THE DIFFERENCE!

The Ten Strategies of Positional Selling in this book focus on *you* and what *you* can do to make that difference. These strategies are not confined to any one particular product, service, or any specific sales arena. They work everywhere.

Energetically employed, these strategies will enable you to create the standard by which all other competitive efforts are judged. *Go for it!*

STRATEGY #1

Take the Lead

My first day in the Marine Corps, I found out the true meaning of the word "subordinate." It didn't take long for a new recruit to discover his place: When the drill sergeant said move, you moved. You didn't question his commands. You didn't think of yourself as an equal. You got used to being kicked around, barked at, and chewed out. The *other* guy was in charge—and you did what he told you.

I didn't like that feeling back then—and I still don't.

And yet, when I went into selling, I carried that same mindset into my new career. It's your job to please the buyer. And when you're sitting on the prayer bench in a drafty lobby alongside three other salespeople all waiting their turn, you *know* who's the subordinate.

YOU ARE!

And you know who's your commanding officer.

IT'S THE BUYER!

But I've got news for you.

Sales relationships that are built like that don't survive the test of time. You aren't going to make it because, first of all, you will become disheartened by what you do, and second, the buyer will lose enthusiasm for you and what you're selling.

When you act like a subordinate, it shows in word and deed.

You apologize for taking up the customer's time. You appear subservient and intimidated. Your expectations hang on his every word because you hope this will be your lucky day, the day he'll give you your big chance.

> SUBORDINATES PRAY FOR MIRACLES
> TO TURN UNFOCUSED SALES CALLS
> INTO LUCKY WINS.

But if you're going to be in position as a salesperson, you don't wait for miracles. A salesperson who's in position becomes a valued resource to the buyer. The value he brings to the customer is the value he brings to the relationship. And you only bring that value if you become an *equal* instead of a *subordinate*.

Taking the lead is absolutely, and without question, the most important first step toward gaining position.

Any time you feel like a subordinate and act it out, I guarantee you, you're out of position. You are *re*active instead of *pro*active. You look to the buyer to take command of the situation instead of *taking the lead for yourself*.

If you can't get excited about what you're selling, how can anyone else? If you don't see yourself as someone who counts for something, your customers will pick up on that, and they won't see you as counting for anything either.

So *how you see yourself* is critical!

I'll never forget a salesman I used to work with named Danny Schorr. Danny was a great guy, but he had all his eggs in one basket—and one day, through no fault of his own, Danny lost his biggest account.

After that, it was curtains for Danny Schorr. He walked around with a dark cloud over his head. Everyone in the office called him "Mr. Mitzelfit." He'd come in and say, "Gee, I don't think I have a chance on this account," or "Do you think they'll buy anything from me today?" It got so bad, people consciously avoided him. They were afraid of becoming infected with his disease, the affliction of *"Ain't it awful!"*

Danny had become his own worst enemy. No one put him in a one-down position. He put himself there. And he was going to stay in that position until he did something to change it.

The fact is, *you decide how successful you're going to be.* If you think self-defeating thoughts and act out those thoughts, the customer will find something wrong with you—and something wrong with what you're selling.

You have to come to grips with the power you have available to you—and use that power to everyone's advantage.

Be confident. Be self-assured. Be knowledgeable. Be assertive.

Use the First Strategy of Positioning: *Take the Lead!*

STRATEGY #2

Stop Looking Out for Number One

Now that we are at the Second Strategy for Positioning, I'm going to define a new pair of words for you. Those words are:

OPERATING REALITY

I'm in my own *operating reality.*
So are you.
We all are.

We're consumed by self-interest. We're obsessed by what's best for *us.* We're protective of our own opinions. Every one of us is *looking out for Number One.*

Now, there's nothing wrong with that. If you happen to be a boxer, a street-fighter, or the sole inhabitant of a tropical island, *looking out for Number One* is the only reasonable approach to take.

But looking out for your own self-interest is not the business of a salesperson. When you're in it just for yourself, and the customer's best interests come second, you may be opting for the short-term gain, the order now, and suffer a long-term loss in the relationship.

THE SALESPERSON IN HIS OWN OPERATING REALITY IS OUT OF POSITION!

When you use the Second Strategy for Positioning, you get out of *your* O.R. and into the *customer's.*

Because if you want to establish an enduring customer relationship, believe me, *it's his reality that matters.*

- What's important to him?
- What need is he trying to satisfy?
- What result is he trying to achieve?

These are going to become the *key issues* in your account relationships.

And you'll have to take steps to understand his Operating Reality that you may never have taken before.

You'll have to know your customer.

You have to understand his values and motivations.

You have to use your heart as well as your head.

You have to sell in terms of *what's important to him* rather than *what's in it for you.*

Or, as a buyer in the garment district used to tell me,

"DON'T TELL ME HOW GOOD YOU MAKE YOUR GOODS. TELL ME HOW GOOD YOUR GOODS MAKE ME."

When you totally immerse yourself in the client's Operating Reality, you *do* climb out of your own skin. His concerns become more important to you than your very own.

Sound impossible?

I'll never forget the example set by some salespeople I trained in Lebanon. These salespeople were from a Middle Eastern conglomerate, Indevco, that marketed baby food, household sanitary supplies, and a wide range of consumer services.

I arrived in Beirut the same week that fighting broke out in the streets—and our training program had to be moved to a hotel in the foothills outside of the city. As the rocket shells and mortar fire burst around us, the salespeople in that room—gathered from all over the Middle East—listened attentively and asked me numerous questions about Positional Selling.

Two years later, when I returned to Beirut, I encountered two of the salesmen who had been in the initial program.

"How are things going?" I asked.

"Very well, Jack," they said. "All things considered, very well. We're very successful in spite of 'the difficulties.' " (Everyone in Beirut referred to the war as "the difficulties.")

As the conversation continued, I learned that both of these salesmen had been taken hostage at one point. After days of negotiations—when neither they, their friends, nor families knew whether they'd get out alive—their company finally paid a ransom to buy their release.

"But why the heck did you go in that area, if you knew there was fighting?" I asked them.

They shrugged. "Well, Jack—*our customers needed us.*"

That conversation is something I'll never forget.

Those Lebanese salesmen weren't *suppliers*.

They were *professional salespeople* in every sense of the word. They were human beings who fully appreciated and understood the needs of other human beings who were counting on them to come through when they were needed.

To me, those sales professionals epitomize the *ideal* and the *reality* of the Second Strategy for Positioning: *They had stopped looking out for Number One!*

STRATEGY #3

Invest in the Relationship

Not long ago, a man who had recently returned from Europe walked into the branch office of one of the largest banks in the Midwest. The gentleman brought with him a check drawn on a German bank that he meant to cash that day.

Unfortunately he had failed to notice the time-limit declaration on the check. By the time he went to cash it, the expiration date had passed. The check was void.

The man was outraged. "What do you mean? No one told me! I *demand* payment! Let me see the manager *at once!*"

He was taken to see the manager—and everyone in the bank braced themselves for a shouting match.

But it didn't turn out that way. The manager listened to his complaint. She acknowledged his frustration—in fact, she agreed that he had every right to *be* frustrated. No, she could not authorize the check to be cashed. But she informed the customer that her bank had a large, active, and highly efficient international department. There was daily courier service to Europe. If the customer agreed to the arrangement, she could return his check by courier to the German bank where it had been issued. And she would request a new check to be drawn A.S.A.P.

The transaction would take a week, at most.

One week later, when the customer came in to pick up his check and cash it, he not only praised the bank manager's handling of the situation, he also apologized for his angry outburst. And because of his interest in the bank's international services (which he hadn't known about before), *he opened a new account!*

Now, there was nothing particularly unusual about this transaction *except* the way it was handled. For the bank manager had used a unique strategy of the Positional Selling process—a strategy I call LAER—to turn the customer's frustration and anger into an opportunity to do business.

LAER is a key Positional Selling strategy. Thousands of salespeople have told me so. *I know* that LAER has had a *significant impact* on their relationships—not only with buyers but also with family, friends, and people within their own organizations.

The Third Strategy for Positioning is more than a way of *overcoming* objections. It's an investment in the relationship. It's a way of putting your own feelings of frustration and exasperation aside and dealing with those of the other person.

LAER is a four-step process model: Listen, Acknowledge, Explore, Respond.

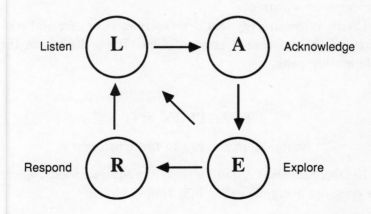

When you use LAER, you *tune in* to the customer instead of tuning him out. With LAER you never need to use those *canned phrases* that give salespeople such a bad reputation. LAER is the strategy that gives you a *window* into the customer's Operating Reality and provides you with a way of responding appropriately so that you begin to see things from the customer's point of view.

But there's something more to LAER—as the example of the irate bank customer indicates.

When you Listen, Acknowledge, Explore, and Respond—sensitively, appropriately, and caringly—something remarkable happens to your relationship with the customer . . . or anyone else.

Anger is defused.

Indifference is replaced by interest.

Impatience is dissipated.

Preoccupation becomes impossible.

Sound like a miracle formula?

It isn't.

When you care enough to listen to another person, to acknowledge that person's concerns, to explore alternatives, and respond to his needs, you are fully in command of a strategy that keeps you in position—*no matter how strong or emotional the customer's distress.*

LAER is the strategy that demonstrates your care and concern for the customer's point of view. It's a deposit in the relationship bank.

STRATEGY #4

Bring Your Energy to the Customer

His real name was Assad Tabib, but in Massachusetts, where he grew up, everyone called him Jimmy Green.

No one who saw him in action *ever* forgot him.

There was a good reason for that.

Jimmy Green swiped stuff off the customers' desks.

The first time I went along with Jimmy Green on a sales call, he leaned over to me and whispered, *"Listen, I want you to steal anything you can get your hands on in the customer's office."*

I said, "What do you want to do that for?"

"Never mind," he said. "Just do what I tell you. Get something off the guy's desk."

So when the customer wasn't looking, I grabbed a pen. As soon as we stepped outside, I gave it to Jimmy.

"O.K.," he said, "now watch me."

We went in to the next customer. Jimmy ceremoniously pulled out the pen and presented it to the customer.

"Carol," he said, "this is a gift from me to you. I want you to keep it as a token of my appreciation for your deep and loyal friendship."

And before we left Carol's office, Jimmy Green stole something different from *her* desk.

So it went throughout the day, swiping something from one buyer to pass on to the next. It took about four months, but eventually you got back what Jimmy Green had *taken off your desk.*

And you know what?

All his customers were in on the scam. It became a joke with them. They used to *love* to see him come. He told stories. He did magic tricks. He stole stuff that didn't come back for a long, long time.

When he walked in to make a sales call, he'd yell:

"I'M HERE!"

People would go *running* into the buyer's office because they wanted to see Jimmy in action. They wanted to be entertained.

Jimmy was the bright spot in a humdrum, dull, and uninteresting day for a lot of people. They used to say to the buyer, "Come on, give him some business. He's the only guy who comes in here and makes us all feel good."

Bizarre? Yes. Effective for Jimmy? Absolutely! Appropriate for everyone? Most certainly not!

The lesson here—Energy! Jimmy brought in a unique kind of excitement to his customers, and they loved it.

ENERGY!!

When it's missing, everyone can tell. I've seen sales calls that were like cigar butts thrown in a water-clogged gutter—dull, soggy, and hard to light.

What they lacked was *energy*.

Energy is *Positive Contact* with the customer. You have to feel good about the people you're calling on. You're hopeful. You're upbeat. You've got a sense of anticipation and expectancy.

And you have to do it your own way. You can't borrow your style from anyone else.

I don't do magic tricks. I don't steal stuff.

But I never go in to a customer without saying to myself, "I'm going to bring this person the best that I can because he doesn't deserve anything less."

I'll bring this customer the best that I have to offer—my *attitude*, my *energy* and my *appearance*.

I'll put on a tuxedo.

I'll get to a boardroom two hours early and move around all the furniture in the room to make sure people know that something exciting is going to happen when they walk in the door.

There are times when I'll go in to a customer and say, *"What's the best thing that could possibly happen to you today?"*

And if he's lost for an answer, I'll ask him, "O.K., what's the *worst* thing that could happen to you today?"

I don't care what it takes—I'm going to keep this relationship and this transaction alive. And we're both going to have fun!

Because buyers get bored.

Salespeople get in a rut. And

A RUT IS A GRAVE WITH THE ENDS KICKED OUT.

If I can't bring my attitude, energy and appearance to the customer, then I don't deserve to be there—I might as well be six feet under.

Sure, it can be risky, but risk-taking is where the action is.

Your *energy* is your *presence*.

And when you *bring your energy* to the customer, you put yourself in position for the best sales call of your career.

Every time.

STRATEGY #5

Get Organized!

Recently I did some consulting work for Bob Santos, the Vice President of Information Management at AT&T.

Bob had an interesting problem that really turned out to be a marvelous opportunity.

Bob's systems analysts were charged with the responsibility of selling their departmental services within the AT&T organization. Even though these systems analysts had an inside edge selling services to their own company, they were encountering stiff outside competition on a fairly consistent basis.

Technically they had a superior product and service.

And their prices were competitive.

But when it came to getting a commitment from the divisions within AT&T, they were failing to achieve their sales objectives.

I was puzzled at first, until I began to interview the management team about their sales goals and strategies. And as I explored further, I realized that most of the company's systems analysts *did not have concrete objectives* for any given sales call.

They were spending a lot of time with the users in a *hit-or-miss mode*. They were telling the users about state-of-the-art technology, but they were not relating that technology to the users' needs.

While their competitors were coming in with a strategy for getting to the point and getting the order, these systems analysts had *no plan* and *no timetable*. They were involved in information-sharing engagements instead of focused, decision-making sales calls.

It wasn't until they got themselves *mentally organized* and *developed a step-by-step sales call plan* that they became the vendor of choice.

It's been estimated that for every hour you spend planning a call, you save three hours of wasted time.

And it's true.

Regrettably, I'm seeing many salespeople today who are less effective than they could be, because they are making six sales calls to accomplish what they should get done in two. And this is understandable, because they have no goal or plan.

The fact is, if you don't know where you're going, *any* road will take you there. You have to decide on an objective, then *plan* the methods and means of achieving that objective.

When a salesperson plans a sales call objective, generates a strategy, and takes action steps for achieving his objectives, he opens the account sooner.

You have to hoard your time and invest it wisely—because your time is a valuable asset.

IN SELLING, THE METER IS ALWAYS RUNNING.

In Positional Selling we use a specific, *written* plan for achieving well-defined objectives within a specific time frame: it's called the *Strategic Selling Plan*.

The Strategic Selling Plan helps you decide:

- Who the decision-makers are—and how you should approach them
- What information you need to have about a customer in order to match your product or service to his needs
- What you hope to accomplish on each sales call
- Your step-by-step activities for accomplishing these goals

With the Strategic Selling Plan, you will avoid making sales calls that have no substance. You revise your timetable so you accomplish more in a shorter loop of time. You plan ahead to trap the future.

Once you get thoroughly organized before every sales call, *you* decide how successful you're going to be!

STRATEGY #6

Find the Area of Opportunity

The Sixth Strategy for Positioning relies on a beautifully simple but effective process for discovering what's important to the customer. It's called the exploratory process.

The exploratory process is the strategy that gets you out of your Operating Reality and into the customer's Operating Reality. (And it sets the stage for the Seventh Strategy for Positioning, *Make the Customer Part of the Solution.*)

In the exploratory process you *ask the right questions* so you can help the customer *discover what he needs.* You find the problem that needs solving, rather than taking your solution around in *search* of a problem.

And believe me, for some salespeople this is quite a departure from their usual approach to selling.

Recently I made a sales call on the senior vice president and the vice president for human resource development at American Fletcher National Bank of Indiana. The officers of American Fletcher were interested in Positional Selling and, as usual, I was prepared to give a thorough presentation with slides, films, and so forth, outlining the value of the program.

But first I wanted to determine *what* our program could do *specifically* to meet the sales development needs of their bank.

My question was phrased in the following manner:

"Gentlemen, before I show you some of the capabilities of the Positional Selling strategies, I would appreciate it if you would tell me something about your organization and what you need to maintain your leadership position in the marketplace."

Then I sat back and listened.

Three and a half hours later, without my making *any kind* of a selling statement or presenting *any kind of information* regarding the content and focus of Positional Selling, the two key players from American Fletcher National Bank were saying things like, "And, Jack, when we implement the Positional Selling strategies, we know our people are going to be more effective in the field and write more business for our bank."

Instead of saying, "This is what I think you must *do*," I'd asked them, "What do you think you *need* to be successful?"

In those three and a half hours, they revealed their need for some very specific sales strategies that they weren't getting at the present time.

In other words, there was a Gap between *where they were now* and *what they were trying to accomplish.*

The Gap is the *area of opportunity.* When you identify the Gap, you can *see* the area of opportunity. You can visualize exactly what needs to be accomplished to satisfy the customer's needs. That's why identifying the Gap is such an important strategy.

With American Fletcher National Bank I took a giant step forward when the vice presidents identified the Gap for me. My job now was simply to bring them the specific elements in Positional Selling that would close that Gap. The remainder of the sales call was devoted to their two questions—how and when they could install Positional Selling within the bank.

The question I had asked was not a random question, by any means.

That question was *meant* to identify the area of opportunity. It asked them to consider the Gap, which looked like this:

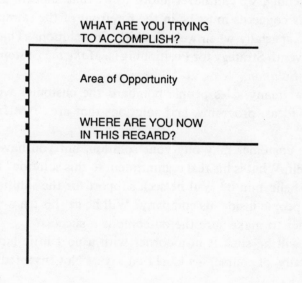

WHAT ARE YOU TRYING
TO ACCOMPLISH?

Area of Opportunity

WHERE ARE YOU NOW
IN THIS REGARD?

By identifying what was important to the customer and what was currently happening, we had discovered a Gap.

And once I had *seen* the Gap, it was easy to close it.

Because that's what salespeople are in business for.

To close Gaps.

And that's what we do with Strategy #7—*Make the Customer Part of the Solution.*

STRATEGY #7

Make the Customer Part of the Solution

In engineering circles, there's a special label for projects that no one wants to work on. They're called "Not Invented Here."

A "Not Invented Here" project is one that ends up with a team of people who don't want it. It isn't theirs. They didn't dream it up. No one has a real, personal commitment to the project. They couldn't care less whether it succeeds or flops.

In selling, we can never afford to let that happen. The customer's concerns must be in the forefront of the salesperson's mind, especially when we're looking for solutions. That's why the Seventh Strategy for Positioning is: *Make the Customer Part of the Solution.*

Now, many sales people bombard the customer with products, ideas, programs, and solutions that are "Not Invented Here."

The customer may buy your solution, but you have to ask yourself: What is his real commitment to this solution? Does he really believe in it? Will he seek support for the solution from other people inside his company? Will he get his team working together to make sure the outcome is a success?

Or will he stick it in a corner with a neat little label on it (mentally, of course)—a label that says, "Not Invented Here"?

Strategy #7 incorporates a model that makes the customer part of the solution by including *his* ideas, *his* needs, and *his* contributions in the presentation. As a matter of fact, by helping you identify a gap, he has already contributed to the development of the solution.

In this strategy, *Make the Customer Part of the Solution,* we use a powerful, action-oriented presentation process called the Diamond. With the Diamond, the customer's assistance is incorporated in the presentation. And time and again throughout the presentation, he's asked to join you in discovering how your solution responds to his needs.

What people commonly perceive to be a monologue turns into a dialogue—a give-and-take process.

The Diamond looks like this:

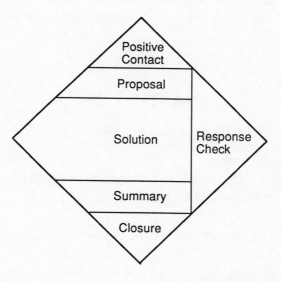

Here's what the model says to you, the salesperson: Every sales call begins with *Positive Contact,* where you bring your energy to the customer. This is followed by a *Proposal*—describing what you hope to accomplish in terms of what's important to the customer. From there, move into the *Solution:* what it is, how it works, and what it will do to benefit the customer and close the Gap. This is followed by the *Summary,* where you emphasize the benefits before moving to *Closure,* when you gain a firm commitment in the form of an order, an agreement, or an action step.

And throughout the presentation, you use the *Response Check* with the customer to make sure you're on track every step of the way.

This model, then, adds structure to your presentation—but without giving you a rigid script to follow. It gives you flexibility to use your own personal style, but at the same time it provides you with a road map to success. With the Diamond, you will never lose your way during the sales call. And the customer recognizes his part in helping you develop the solution.

STRATEGY #8

Assume the Responsibility

You're the expert.

It's not up to the buyer to manage all the dynamics involved in the sales process. It's up to *you.*

YOU CONTROL YOUR OWN BEHAVIOR.

And your behavior will influence the buying decision.
More than price.
More than technical knowledge.
More than capability statements.
Unless you are selling a much-needed, unique product that

cannot be obtained from any other source, the buying decision will be based upon:

WHO YOU ARE
HOW YOU BEHAVE
WHAT YOU SAY
HOW YOU SAY IT AND
WHEN YOU SAY IT

But not all salespeople are alike, as we know.

And, certainly, not all customers are alike.

That's why it's so important to *Assume the Responsibility.*

To achieve that goal, *you* have to be flexible in using the Gap to identify the area of opportunity and using the Diamond to make the customer part of the solution. That means you have to be absolutely ready, if necessary, to change your tactics—even in the middle of the transaction—so that you can respond to the changing dynamics of the sales call.

Some time ago, I was making a call with an outstanding sales professional—Jimmy Greer, who was representing Iowa Beef Processors. Iowa Beef is a company that provides precut, packaged beef products to supermarket chains.

I was fortunate to accompany him one day during a call on Stanley Moravitz, the vice president of merchandising for the Giant Eagle Supermarket chain.

Upon our arrival, the vice president's secretary informed us that we would have to wait. Mr. Moravitz, she said, was downtown getting his passport picture in preparation for a three-week vacation in Rome and Israel.

When Mr. Moravitz finally came in, he apologized for the delay and invited us into his office. Jimmy Greer broke the ice by asking him about the upcoming vacation.

Then Jimmy launched into his presentation. "Well, Mr. Moravitz, when we met several weeks ago, I said I would like to return and present you with some ideas that I believe can help you save money and help you run a more efficient and profitable meat department. And I'm here today to do just that."

"O.K., fellas," Mr. Moravitz said, glancing at his watch. "Go ahead. What have you got?"

Greer started telling him what the Iowa Beef Processors program was, how it worked, and what it would do for Giant Eagle. But as Jimmy got about five or six selling statements into his presentation, I was interested to observe that *it appeared as if Mr. Moravitz had fallen asleep!*

His body was present. But his mind was elsewhere—far away on the balmy shores of a Mediterranean beach.

One glance told me that Mr. Moravitz was suffering from brain drift.

Suddenly Jimmy Greer *stopped his presentation.*

"Mr. Moravitz!"

"Huh?" Mr. Moravitz sat up.

"Mr. Moravitz, I've been telling you all about boxed beef, but I'm not so sure I'm doing the right thing. So, instead of *me* telling *you* any more, let me ask you a question:

"What is important to you when you consider a boxed beef program? What does a program like that have to do to *help you achieve your objectives* as the head of the Giant Eagle meat department?"

Then Jimmy Greer shut his mouth!

For the next twenty minutes, we heard all about it. Mr. Moravitz said, I need *this, this, and this.* And when Greer had his chance, he sold Mr. Moravitz on how the Iowa Beef Processors boxed beef program could give him the benefits he was looking for.

"Mr. Moravitz," he concluded, "when can I begin to help you improve your productivity here in the meat department at Giant Eagle?"

And Mr. Moravitz made a significant commitment to the installation of Iowa Beef's Cattle Pack within Giant Eagle.

Flexibility.
It's the key.
Jimmy Greer was able to move from a *presentation posture* into an *exploratory posture,* and back to a presentation posture. He read the signs and called a change of play. In football terms, he *called an audible*—just as a quarterback does when he changes a play on the line of scrimmage.

Rather than sticking to his original sales call strategy of presenting a solution, he shifted gears, re-established Giant Eagle's needs, and moved back into presenting benefits once again. He steered the transaction in a *new* direction, then got it back to the *original* direction.

Jimmy Greer *could* have let the sales call dribble off the edge of the table as Stanley Moravitz went into a comatose state.

Instead, Jimmy Greer assumed responsibility for the leadership role and altered his *own* behavior. By being attentive and flexible, he responded to the changing dynamics of the sales transaction. He did the right thing at the right time.

STRATEGY #9

Put It in Writing

In many sales arenas, an immediate response to your order-asking question may go something like this:

"We're going to have to think it over. We have many other matters to consider in relation to your proposal presentation."

Those other matters include competitive offers, advice from other people, and internal discussions around the product and service you're offering.

For some salespeople, the next job after this kind of response is to *wait and pray.*

To that I say—*Malarkey!*

Now the real selling job begins. The activities you engage in between the conclusion of the face-to-face transaction and the announcement of the buying decision cannot be mope-and-hope activities.

For the heads-up salesperson, *this* is the time to *pursue, pursue, pursue!*

During a recent cutback at a large New England corporation, the human resource development department of the company was approached by Maryann Ramirez, an independent job placement counselor and sole proprietor of her own company called MACGIL, Inc.

After an extensive needs analysis, Maryann made a detailed presentation outlining a two-year career-path planning program for the corporation's soon-to-be-terminated employees.

After Maryann made her presentation, the HRD people said they would talk about it and get back to her. They made it clear that they were in the process of considering several competitive proposals—and they would not commit themselves to a date for an answer.

The evening after her presentation, Maryann prepared a *summary sales proposal* detailing everything she had discussed. ("I wasn't sure how much they would remember after I walked out of there," she explained.) Her written proposal presented an accurate picture of everything that happened on the sales call—and it served as a constant reminder of something they could react to.

After the proposal was delivered—the day following the meeting—Maryann followed up with a number of phone calls centered around: "Did you receive my proposal? Do you have any reactions to it? How do you see it working within the organization? What is its status? May I have the opportunity to implement all the benefits it contains?"

As it turned out, Maryann Ramirez was *the only consultant* who put her sales presentation in writing. That proposal—and the implementation of follow-up strategies—gave her the competitive edge.

It set her apart from the rest.

And she got the business.

The Ninth Strategy of Positional Selling is all those things you do *after* the sales call to make sure that you stay in the buyer's consciousness. It is a strategy that encompasses every facet of your post-call activities, from the proposal you write to the phone calls you make.

It means *never* taking yourself out of position.

It means *always* maintaining a presence.

It means pursuing the right people at the right time in the right ways—you set a standard of professionalism that no one else can match.

STRATEGY #10

Become the Only Choice!

I believe that by the end of this book, you're going to have some clear alternatives.

You can try *none* of the strategies of Positional Selling.

You can try *some* of them.

Or you can try *all* of them.

In the pages that follow, I will provide you with the details of the Ten Strategies—but it's up to you to put them together into one dynamic presentation. You have to dig in and see how each strategy relates to your selling environment. You will have to experiment with these concepts and make them a part of you.

How you use these strategies will depend upon your style, your personality, your values, and your uniqueness. *These* are the dominant factors in selling. The concepts, attitudes, and models are merely a framework to help you position yourself. I urge you to shape them to your purpose, your needs, and the vision of your personal goals.

Recently, I was talking about selling with a friend of mine, Mike Shaeffer, who has been using the Positional Selling strategies for a number of years.

Throughout the time I've known him, Mike has been one of the hardest working and most dedicated salespeople I've ever met. He is constantly reviewing his past sales activities and seeking to *improve*. Every time we have a conversation, he focuses on what he can do to better his performance—and once he has made his decision, he makes a conscious effort to *implement* those improvements.

The last time we were together, I asked him, "Mike, what has been the most rewarding experience for you as a salesperson?" He thought for a moment before he replied. "Jack," he said, "it's something that happens all the time. But it only *began* to happen after I started using Positional Selling.

"Frequently, when the phone rings," he continued, "I realize that I know *who* is on the phone, I know *why* that person is calling, and I have a pretty good idea *what* he's going to say. The first couple of times this happened, I gave myself a pat on the back for guessing right.

"But now I know it's not guesswork—and that's a great feeling. Everything I've done for weeks or months leads up to that call. I know exactly *when* I'm going to get a commitment because *any other alternative is out of the question.*

"Jack, there's no big mystery to this. It's just a matter of doing the right thing and doing it right." He laughed. "And if I'm not doing it right *yet*—I keep trying."

The Tenth Strategy for Positioning focuses on that final phone call—the one that comes *when* you expect it, giving you the *commitment you deserve* from a person whose *trust in you is well-justified.* When you are doing everything right, you set the stage for that predictable decision on the part of the customer.

When the customer makes a commitment, *it must be to you.*

You *create the ability* to predict outcomes, because in the customer's eyes, you have *become* the only choice.

And when you ask for the order, you'll never get no for an answer.

3

The First Strategy for Positioning:
Take the Lead

A good friend of mine, who later became one of the top sales professionals for the Dixon Paper Company, got his start some time ago selling toilet paper to hotels and motels in the Denver area.

On his first day, Loren Wilson called on the Bugs Bunny Hotel on Colfax Avenue on the west side of Denver.

As with most salespeople on their first call, he was flying blind. He had no idea what to say to the buyer.

Armed with product knowledge but very few selling skills, he took his marching orders and hit the road.

So there was Loren in his car with a back seat full of toilet paper samples and not the slightest notion of how to approach his prospective buyer.

He drove around the Bugs Bunny Hotel *four times* before he finally got out of the car with a sample and strode inside.

"I'd like to see the manager," he declared to the clerk at the front desk.

"What about?" she asked him.

Loren cleared his throat. "I have some—hotel supplies I'd like to show him."

The clerk disappeared for a few moments, then returned. "He'll be out in a minute."

Nearly a half-hour went by. Finally a door opened and the hotel manager appeared.

Loren leaped to his feet. Before the manager could open his mouth, Loren delivered the selling presentation that he had been contemplating for the past half-hour:

"Say," he said, *"you don't want to buy any toilet paper today, do you?"*

The manager looked at him for a moment and then said, "You're right, I don't."

This story would be funny if it weren't so typical.

Unfortunately, too many salespeople are in just this position when they start out. They have a good understanding of their product, but they don't know how to convince the customer to buy it. So they wind up feeling insecure, not fit for the job, powerless—and as a result, subordinate to the people they are calling on.

When a salesperson feels like a subordinate, count on him to act it out. His relationship to the buyer looks like this:

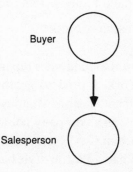

not like this:

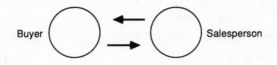

He uses the *language of a loser:*

"I don't want to take much of your time, but . . ."

"I know you're busy, so I'll make it quick."

"Take your time—I've got all day."

"I'll be glad to come back later when you have more time."

"Would it be all right if I covered these ideas with you today?"

Around the office, before making a sales call, he will be heard to say:

"I don't know if it will work."

"I don't think they will like it."

"What if they consider the price too high?"

"I wish I didn't have to show this idea to his partner."

"If only I could catch a break!"

When I was a commissioned sales rep in the familiar environs of midtown New York, I used to go through a *voice change* between Sunday afternoon and Monday morning. On Saturdays and Sundays I was a company commander in the Marine Corps reserve in Garden City, New York. I spoke with authority and confidence. I had a Patton-style baritone that I exercised in front of the H&S Company, Second Battalion, 25th Marines: "Gunnery Sergeant Henson! Prepare the company for inspection!"

On Monday morning, what a change! I turned into a canary. My voice was soprano. "Oh, good morning, Mr. Martorana. I don't suppose I could have some of your time, could I?"

Needless to say, it was more than a change of voice that I went through between Sunday and Monday. When I appeared in front of the buyer on Monday morning, my confidence was shot. I felt like a person without skills, talent, or ability. I played the role of subordinate because I *felt* like a subordinate.

In sales, no one gave me a pat on the back and told me I was doing a great job, for the very simple reason that I *wasn't*. I *couldn't*. I didn't know how!

WHAT'S YOUR WORKING IMAGE OF YOURSELF?

This is a question you have to answer before you can take the first step toward positioning yourself as an effective salesperson.

Positioning is more than an external state. It's also an *internal* state. How you feel about yourself and how you evaluate your own strengths will ultimately have a loud and clear impact on the customer. So before you can work on all the things that go into a results-producing sales call, you have to get a firm grip on your own positive qualities and see yourself as counting for something.

You need to have *Inner Position*—the firm conviction that you are a valuable asset to the customer and everyone else you come in contact with.

There are many things that can stand in the way of achieving Inner Position, and I'll talk about some of them later. But I think it's important to recognize, first of all, that Inner Position plays a huge role in determining your relationship with others.

How you see yourself always affects how you will relate to other people.

Who's a subordinate?

Many salespeople are in a subordinate position to their customers because they *see themselves* as lacking power and influence. This is an easy trap to fall into. But in order to have a healthy, give-and-take relationship with the customer, you have to turn a subordinate relationship into a relationship of equality.

This is tough to do when the cards are stacked against you. You are constantly asking for things and the customer has the option of saying "yes" or "no." Here are just some of the things you ask for:

- An appointment with the customer
- The customer's time
- Information
- That he be open to your ideas
- That he trust and believe in you
- A commitment

And every time you ask for something, you set yourself up for being turned down. You're in a subordinate position with the customer who is holding the ace in the hole. Naturally you are in a dependency posture.

Furthermore, there are always some customers who will *remind* you of their power, every chance they get. When you have a customer like that, it's easy to see him as an adversary. The customer becomes the enemy and the sales arena a battleground. But the harder you fight, the more domineering the customer becomes—until it's a standoff.

How do you *change* that situation? How do you transform a dominant–subordinate relationship into a relationship of equality?

Many salespeople think it's up to the customer to make that change. We say things like, "He's going to give me some slack." "He's softening up." "He is going to give me a break." "I've got the edge on him now."

But it's not the customer's responsibility to improve the quality of the relationship. That change must be brought about by you. And to do that, you will have to change how you see yourself.

Some time ago, I was conducting a sales seminar for Plastic Piping Systems in Chicago. Midway through the seminar, I said to the participants, "I want you to do a little exercise for me. I want each one of you in this room to think of three things you like most about yourself. Just three things. You can write them down or just hold those thoughts in your head, but I want you to concentrate very clearly on those three things. O.K.?"

I gave them a moment to think, then I asked, "Now, who wants to tell me three things you like about yourself?"

No hands went up, of course, so I said, "O.K., I'll start it off. Here are the three things that I really like about myself."

And that broke the ice. After that we began to go around the room, and sure enough, hands went up and people began to participate.

Suddenly a young woman who was sitting in the middle row got up and rushed out of the room. I continued the discussion, but during the next break, I went out to talk to her.

When I found her, she was visibly upset. "Jack," she volunteered, "I'm sorry I left the room like that. But when you asked that question, I realized there wasn't *anything* about myself I liked."

About two years later, I had the occasion to encounter the same young woman. During the intervening time, I'd heard that she was doing very well.

When I saw her again, I asked, "What's working for you *now* that wasn't working back then?"

"Jack," she said, "the difference is I *believe* in myself. I've come to the realization that in the final analysis, *I'm* the one responsible for my own self-image."

As we talked further, I began to realize what had been the actual cause of this talented young woman's low self-esteem.

She was acutely sensitive to feelings of rejection. She overpersonalized any form of negative feedback and set herself up to be the target. The most insignificant comment from a customer would have a devastating effect on her. She couldn't handle the kinds of rejection that salespeople hear all the time in words such as:

"I'm sorry, I don't have time to see you today."

"Your price is way too high. We can't even consider a purchase."

"I've talked with our V.P. of purchasing and we've decided against it."

"I'm afraid your proposal just doesn't have what we're looking for."

Every time a prospect or customer says words to this effect, a salesperson has to deal with the consequences. Hearing "no" is bad enough. Letting it paralyze you is even worse. There's no reason why rejection needs to be a severe setback to your emotional health—yet for many salespeople, it's just that.

People in sales live in a winner-oriented society. We don't get any reward for losing, so we fight rejection on two fronts—our own disappointment in ourselves and others' disappointment in us.

Yet, as hard as we fight, we may suffer from "rejection hangover." We've heard "no" so many times that we take it to heart.

We develop self-doubting attitudes that deplete our energy and seriously inhibit our effectiveness.

Nothing is more strength-sapping than the low spirits that accompany rejection. If you hold on to the feelings and dwell on them, they can cripple you.

Elisabeth Kübler-Ross, M.D., in her book *On Death and Dying,* identified a number of "levels of grieving." I have taken the liberty and poetic license of explaining these levels of grieving as they affect salespeople, and added a few of my own.

Whenever we are set back by disappointment, failure, rejection, or loss, we go through a series of emotional states that affect us in the following ways:

Shock. The bad news leaves you mentally immobilized. You are temporarily disoriented, confused, and angry. The feeling of loss or rejection is painful. Especially if it takes you by surprise.

Denial. It's so bad that you refuse to accept reality. You deny the event happened. You may even escape into fantasy by imagining all the good feelings that *would* surround you if the loss had never occurred.

Blaming. You incriminate yourself for not having taken proper or decisive action. Or you blame others for not having given you the support, attention, or assistance that you needed.

Acceptance. You finally accept what's happened. There's nothing you can do about it except learn from the experience.

Renewal. You put the past aside and prepare for what's ahead. Renewal shows your bounce-back ability and your resilience. You refocus your thoughts and look ahead to the future. You get on with your life.

At one time or another, all of us have been through each of these emotional levels. If we could say what we feel, this is what we would hear:

Shock: "I am stunned by the 'no.' "

Denial: "I don't believe I didn't get the order."

Blaming: "If only I had been more competitive."

Acceptance: "How can I learn from losing?"

Renewal: "This is what I am going to do to win."

Holding on to feelings of shock, denial, and blaming every time you get a "no" can wear you down emotionally. When you add these feelings up over a period of time, the sum total is self-doubt and a subordinate reaction.

We must go through these self-defeating emotional states and move ahead to acceptance and renewal as rapidly as possible.

If you have a plan for recovery, you can bounce back from rejection and disappointment by mobilizing your inner resources and putting them into action.

Your ability to go through shock, denial, and blaming is in direct proportion to your individual sense of self-esteem. If your current working image of yourself is in the pits, then you will find it more difficult to move from shock to renewal.

You can start the process of creating Inner Position by claiming your strengths and valuing yourself.

By being good to yourself, you will be good to others. It's an intelligent kind of selfishness.

ASK YOURSELF

How do you see yourself? What qualities are working *for* you? Take a moment to consider some personal qualities that you bring to your customer relationships. What are the qualities that apply to you?

_____ I get along well with people.
_____ I am persistent.
_____ I share my enthusiasm.
_____ I can be trusted to do my best.
_____ I have a wealth of new ideas.
_____ I am a hard worker.
_____ I'm confident that I'm a success.
_____ I give credit to people who help me achieve my goals.
_____ I am knowledgeable about what I'm selling.
_____ I understand what people want to achieve.

Now consider the way these personal qualities have helped your professional performance in the past. Think about a recent sales achievement. The last time you got a commitment from a customer, what were the deciding factors in the relationship? What three things helped sway the buying decision in your favor?

_____ I built a strong, supportive bond with the customer.
_____ I refused to give up until I got the order.
_____ My enthusiasm lit a fire.
_____ The customer came to trust me.
_____ I brought in new ideas that helped solve the customer's problems.
_____ I earned respect through hard work.
_____ I made the customer feel successful along with me.
_____ By sharing credit with people, I made them look good, too.
_____ The customer respected my product knowledge.
_____ The customer was grateful that I achieved results for him.

ACTION STEPS

But what if you *aren't* feeling good about yourself right now? What if you've just taken a hard knockdown, and you're still suffering the consequences of shock, denial, and blaming?

Recovering from the rejection hangover is more than a process of hoping and praying. You have to be straight with yourself. And you have to take positive action steps, starting with giving yourself a "self talk":

1. Remind yourself of the good things you have accomplished for your customers recently. Make a mental list to keep those accomplishments at the forefront of your mind.
2. Think long range. Don't be devastated by early setbacks. You'll be around for a long time and you'll get a second, third, fourth, and many more chances.
3. Confide in a good friend. Solicit positive feedback. Ask that friend, "Why would you buy from me?" Rub shoulders with this person and get well.
4. Remember that the customer can't say "no" forever. If you're persistent and he sees you trying, he'll help you find a way to win with him.
5. Ask yourself what did I learn from losing the order this time? And how do I plan to be better the next time out?

POSITIVE IMAGING

One way to turn a subordinate relationship into a relationship of equality is through positive imaging. Think of all the things that could turn out right on every sales call. Imagine them vividly, completely, and in great detail—so you're prepared for the very best outcome.

1. Look forward with anticipation to every sales call, as a great event and celebration of your ability to help the customer.
2. See yourself as being more knowledgeable, better prepared, and more decisive than your competitors.
3. See yourself as looking fit, performing well, and having the durability to see things through to a conclusion.
4. See yourself as capable of responding to the customer's needs.
5. Imagine yourself enjoying the rewards accompanying a successful sales call, rewards such as:

- The customer's trust and regard for you
- The respect and recognition of your associates
- The sense of pride for having accomplished your goal

Put a New Message in Your Head

Have a talk with yourself. Fill your conversation with strong, positive words. It's only when you convince yourself you are O.K. that you can convince others. Tell yourself:

"I only know of one way to do things—and that's the best way I know how."

"I'm going to have an objective and a strategy for making every sales call pay off. I'm determined to define what's important to the customer. I'm going to respond with concrete solutions. I will ask for a commitment to action."

"I know my stuff."

"I can handle 'no.' "

"I bring value to the relationship."

When you have these messages in your head on every sales call, you have taken charge of yourself and you will take the lead. These are the messages that help you establish Inner Position and make you the customer's equal in your eyes and his.

When you are an equal, your words reflect confidence, self-respect, and a recognition of your own worth. These are not words that you can memorize. You can't *create* a sense of self-worth unless you truly value yourself and bring your value to the relationship.

When you do, the words will come naturally. They will reflect the fact that you regard yourself as a worthy decision-maker in a position of shared and equal power. You will never let yourself down. And above all, you will possess the emotional stamina to handle temporary setbacks.

It's only when you feel confident of your own position, strength, and abilities that you can take the next important step toward establishing a bond with the customer. And that's when you:

STOP LOOKING OUT FOR NUMBER ONE.

4

The Second Strategy for Positioning:
Stop Looking Out for Number One

Imagine, for a moment, that you are the customer.

A salesperson comes to see you. He seems likable, enthusiastic, and knowledgeable. You take to him immediately.

But, after you've been talking for a couple of minutes, you notice the salesperson is not listening. He has that faraway look in his eyes. And the minute you take a breath, he leaps into a canned sales pitch that has nothing whatever to do with what you were saying:

"I'm glad you mentioned that, Jack, because we have exactly what you're looking for. In fact, I've got the solution for you! I guarantee you, if you just take a moment to look at my plan, the problems you're experiencing right now will disappear!"

And with that introduction, the salesperson launches directly into a very energetic presentation that doesn't have the slightest bearing on what you really need.

Self-centered salespeople are not uncommon. Their primary purpose is to create a universe of customers to serve their own self-interests.

Salespeople like this are incapable of any professional relationship in which they are not the centerpiece and the dominant figure. Salespeople who fill this mold just can't see things from the customer's point of view. They block their understanding of the other person's world because they are so concerned with their own. They have a tape running through their head that says:

"WHAT'S IN IT FOR ME?"

They're concerned with telling a good story. They think the customer's activity should be confined to that of an attentive listener who's going to hear them out and then *buy in* to the solution.

This is the kind of salesperson who's always looking out for Number One.

Some years ago, I conducted an extensive survey throughout North America, South America, Europe, and the Middle East. The purpose of our survey was to find out how salespeople typically react in a variety of stressful sales situations—dealing with complaints, handling objections, and working with resistance. We surveyed a substantial population of salespeople representing diverse products and services, and we conducted follow-up interviews with the participants. Their industries included automobile sales, real estate, insurance, and every variety of industrial sales.

In designing the survey, we asked ourselves two questions:

1. How does the customer's message *affect* the salesperson?
2. Upon receiving that message, what is the salesperson's first reaction?

The results were conclusive. The survey responses clearly showed that:

1. When a salesperson hears a customer's message, the odds are *two to one* that he interprets that message in terms of *how it affects himself.*
2. The odds are *two to one* that the salesperson's first action after receiving that message will be a self-centered reaction rather than a customer-centered response.

In other words, this survey indicates that most of the time, you're hearing the customer's words in terms of how his concerns affect you personally. Your understanding of his meaning is clouded by your self-centered orientation. You express your frustrations and your helplessness, your unfounded assumptions, your preoccupation with what's in it for you, and your impatience with wanting to conclude the transaction and get the order.

All of these concerns are part of what I call a person's *Operating Reality.*

What is Operating Reality?

A person's O.R. is the sum total of his assumptions, values, motivations, and predispositions—all the things that cause him to act in certain ways.

A salesperson's Operating Reality screens out what the customer says to find out what's in it for the salesperson. It's a little like panning for gold. The only thing you look for in the pan of gravel is that which will put money in your pocket.

A customer's Operating Reality is composed of his needs to solve current problems, prevent future problems, increase efficiency, improve productivity, reduce hassles, and achieve a greater sense of well-being. He wants to know how the salesperson can help him achieve his goals.

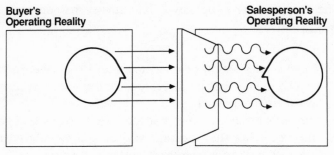

Buyer's Operating Reality

Salesperson's Operating Reality

Filtered Communication

"This is what I need to solve my problems and achieve my goals."

"How does what he's saying affect what I'm trying to accomplish during this sales call?"

When a salesperson is completely caught up in his own Operating Reality instead of the customer's Operating Reality, he fails to deal with what's important to the customer.

As one salesperson said to me, "You know, Carew, I believe that salespeople are caught up in their own O.R. a lot of the time. They're only interested in how what-is-happening is going to affect them, regardless of how it's going to affect the customer." And he continued, "Carew, of the salespeople I know who are caught up in their *own* O.R., I'd guess *eighty percent* don't give a damn about the customer's problems, and the other *twenty percent* are *glad he has them!*"

Now, the key to creating position with the customer is somehow to get out of your O.R. and into his O.R. And it takes a conscious effort to do that—to walk in the door and say, "I'm going to make an effort to pay attention to what this person has to say. I'm going to *learn* a lot by listening to him and I'm probably going to get the kind of data that I need to make this a productive sales call."

So you have to reprogram yourself to get out of *your* Operating Reality and into the *buyer's* reality—and that's not easy. But it's in the buyer's Operating Reality where the decisions are made.

Buyer's Operating Reality

Salesperson in Buyer's Operating Reality

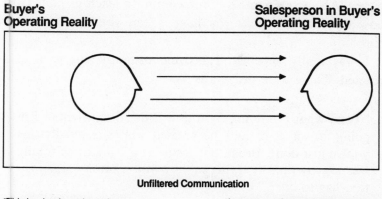

Unfiltered Communication

"This is what I need to solve my problems and achieve my goals."

"I want to understand what the buyer needs so I can help him solve his problems and achieve his goals."

A recent experience of my own underscores the difficulty of making this transition—and it cost me precious time and money.

The incident occurred when I was making a sales call on one of Ireland's preeminent banking institutions in Dublin. I had set up an appointment with one of the bank's personnel officers—the person who bought training programs, set up lectures, and invited outside professors and facilitators to train the bank personnel.

I had just arrived in Ireland the day before and I was still rebounding from the effects of jet lag. In addition, I had several other key appointments planned for the two days I was in Dublin. Having missed a night's sleep, I was anxious about being at my best. I'd been forewarned that trying to sell something to this Irish bank was like making a one-thousand-mile turn—you had to be very patient.

The gentleman kept me waiting approximately a half-hour. He arrived at his office long after I was there, cleared up some personal business, and then came out to greet me.

After a few pleasantries, the first words out of his mouth

were, "Ah, here's another Yank comin' to teach us poor Irish how to *sell*. I suppose you have a film you want to show me?"

I was really shocked. I became instantly angry. And I reacted. These were my words:

"Tom, what I'm doing right now is deciding whether I'm going to sit here and be treated unprofessionally—as you've just done. Because it seems as if I might be totally wasting my time by trying to show you what my organization has to offer."

He tried to laugh it off: "Ah, touchy, touchy, touchy."

"No, Tom," I went on. "I just don't feel good about what you just said."

Well, needless to say, the sales call went downhill from that point on. He gave me the time he'd promised—about an hour and a half—but we never really connected as people. And that was because I blew my stack and I *reacted*.

I could have said:

"Tom, I regret that you feel this way. However, I am really here to identify your training needs and respond in a responsible way."

But I didn't say that. Instead, I resorted to delivering a verbal knuckle sandwich.

An hour and a half later, I wound up in a Baggot Street pub—consuming a pint of Guinness Stout while I nursed the awful feeling of blowing that sales call in a big way.

The way I *failed* on that call was by not understanding Tom's Operating Reality.

For example, there were lots of unanswered questions.

Was Tom reflecting on the aftereffects of a bad experience

he'd had with sales training programs in the past? Did he mistrust American salespeople? And if so, for what reason? What was his experience with American business? Did he currently have an effective training program for the bank's calling officers?

I also had to consider the delay in our meeting. What had caused it? Had Tom intended to be late for the appointment? Or had he been legitimately delayed? Was he *really* sending me a "signal" by making me wait?

And what about his situation in the bank? Had he introduced a program in the past that didn't work? Was he under the gun to produce and become more effective? Was he protecting other people within his organization who might be threatened by my training proposal?

If I had gathered *any* of this data, I might have turned that meeting into a productive sales call. Finding out what *prompted* his introductory remark would have taken me a lot closer to understanding who he was and what he wanted.

But by focusing on my own anger, I closed off the avenues of information. And instead of building a feeling of trust, I made him defensive and cautious.

Throughout that meeting, he was wary of me. Given my self-centered reaction to his first remark, he had every right to remain that way.

In getting out of your own Operating Reality and into the customer's Operating Reality, the key strategy is listening.

YOU HAVE TO LISTEN!

And I don't mean listening to *win.* I mean listening to *understand.*

Some time ago I was the after-dinner speaker before a sales group at the New York Athletic Club. My talk was about *listening.* I wanted to emphasize that I considered listening a key strategy in developing position with a customer.

Throughout the talk, I was saying things like, "Listening is the best way to say you care"; "Listening is paying attention to the other person as a human being"; and "Listening means taking the other person seriously."

I ended the talk on a highly motivational note—and received a very receptive round of applause. But when the emcee asked for questions from the floor, one salesman (who'd obviously been imbibing heavily) staggered to his feet and announced:

"I don't have any questions. But I'd like to say something."

"I'd be very interested in what you have to say," I urged.

"Well, I'd like to say that *good listeners are garbage dumps!*"

There was an immediate uproar—the audience was laughing and pounding on tables.

And I really didn't know what to say. I was completely at a loss.

Just then another hand shot up in the back of the room and a second salesman got to his feet.

"Mr. Speaker, I'd like to make a statement."

Like my first critic, the second looked and sounded as if he'd had a few too many.

Still smarting from the previous remark, I managed, "I'd be delighted to hear what you have to say, sir."

"I agree with this other gentlemen!" he pronounced. "Good listeners *are* garbage dumps. However, I'd like to add something: *Better listeners are recycling centers!*"

And there was a *thunderous* round of applause from the audience.

On reflection, I think there was a lot of wisdom in that grandstand pronouncement. I believe what he was saying is this: If you are a *committed* listener—a listener who's attempting to help another person—you may become the very means by which that person rebuilds or recycles himself or his life.

You take something that's initially negative and, by listening, help that person *turn it into something good.*

So, yes. I agree. Good listeners are garbage dumps.

But *better* listeners are recycling centers.

The trouble is, much of our listening is *contaminated* by self-interest. Often we place our *own* meaning on what we hear rather than *listening to understand* what the other person is trying to say.

That happens to a great degree with salespeople. The buyer says something and the salesperson draws a different meaning. Each of them is in his own Operating Reality—and mutual understanding of the problem does not occur. By the time a message reaches your brain, it has *your* meaning rather than the meaning that was intended by the buyer.

One Sunday when my wife and I were attending services, our pastor was on a roll. His topic was "Forgiving and Forgetting." Midway through his sermon, he got around to saying:

"Husbands, if you keep reminding your wife of her faults and mistakes and little inadequacies, you haven't forgiven because you haven't forgotten.

"And wives, the same is true for you. If you keep reminding your husband that he forgot your birthday, didn't pick up the dry cleaning, and didn't put gas in the car, you haven't forgiven because you haven't forgotten."

I was hanging on the pastor's every word. When the pastor came to this point in the sermon, I leaned over to my wife and whispered, "Barbara, I hope you're paying attention to what he has to say."

And she shot back—loud enough that I could hear quite clearly—"Yes, because he's talking about *you!*"

Now, it was very clear to me that my wife *did not hear the same message* that I heard.

Each of us only heard what we *wanted* to hear. I was hearing what would support *my* point of view and *my* feelings. And my wife was hearing support for *her* point of view and *her* feelings.

Each of us has our own Operating Reality.

And until we dislodge ourselves from what's important to *us* and get ourselves into the other person's O.R., we fail to connect as two people. We fail to understand and respond.

TO BE IN YOUR OWN O.R. IS HUMAN NATURE.
TO GET INTO ANOTHER PERSON'S O.R. IS HUMAN
RELATIONS.

How do you go about understanding your customer's O.R.? You have to consider that person's needs, priorities, and motivations:

- For a consumer purchasing an appliance, what's important to her may be ease of operation, no maintenance, greater efficiency, and less fatigue in accomplishing chores around the house.
- For a person purchasing an automobile, it could be saving money on gas mileage, greater comfort, and the prestige of owning a luxury machine.
- For a person purchasing a life insurance policy, it could be the need for guaranteed future financial security, and providing for a child's education.
- For a professional purchasing agent, it could be solving a productivity problem, increasing effectiveness in his plant operation, and saving his company money.

The secret to being a very good sales professional—the secret to initiating, establishing, and building position—is always to be in the customer's Operating Reality.

What barriers prevent you from working with the customer's Operating Reality?

I believe there are four:

ANGER

INDIFFERENCE

IMPATIENCE

PREOCCUPATION

When I met with the bank officer in Ireland, my reaction showed all four of these:

Anger because I was kept waiting.

Indifference because no matter how Tom felt about us "Yanks," I wanted him to be receptive to what I was selling.

Impatience because he was blocking the way I wanted the sales call to go.

Preoccupation because I was battling fatigue and was distracted by my busy schedule.

Selling is replete with choices and consequences. If you *choose* self-centered reactions, the consequences are predictable—and in most cases have the potential to damage what you're trying to achieve.

By reacting with Anger, Indifference, Impatience, and Preoccupation at the bank in Dublin, I closed the door to an opportunity.

Every time you allow these reactions to control your behavior, you lose the opportunity to build a relationship with a customer.

But there are steps you can take to overcome self-centered

reactions and build customer-centered *responses.* When you understand the effects your reactions have on the customer, you are in a better position to make more productive choices.

SIGNS OF ANGER

For some salespeople, a day of sales calls is a series of one angering encounter after another.

"Don't waste your time calling on me, your organization is not qualified to handle our business."

"I can't see you now, I am busy, and I haven't got time to spend with you."

"I decided to give the business to your competitor for the following reasons . . ."

Having things happen like:

- Being kept waiting in a drafty lobby for an inordinate amount of time, especially after making a confirmed appointment
- Having a customer renege on an order that was promised to you
- Being lied to and manipulated
- Being let down by your own organization and not supported by your manager

For some salespeople, events like these are a daily staple in the emotional diet of our occupation.

Add up these defeating events over a period of time and it's no wonder that irritation, frustration, and stress set in. The result is anger.

Overcoming Anger

Acknowledge your anger. Humor yourself. Say, "That's the way it goes." You'll be able to take anger in stride and defuse its effects. Prove to yourself that you are stronger than the anger you are feeling.

Postpone the pleasure. Fulton J. Sheen once said, "Maturity is the ability to postpone pleasure." When it comes to dealing with anger, postpone the pleasure it would give you to put the offender in his place. Postponement of pleasure gives you a greater sense of personal power and control.

Try kindness. It earns restraint. On occasion, you will encounter a customer whose anger with you seems excessive in light of the severity of the problem. Many times this anger is an accumulation of negative experiences that have happened to this person over the course of the day, and you become the target. Manage your anger, and allow the customer to blow off steam. By showing genuine concern for him as a person, you may cause an exciting reversal. The customer may begin to treat you with the same regard that you're treating him.

I've seen it occur numerous times. The customer gets it out of his system. If you have the stamina to endure his harangue, the air will be cleared by itself. He'll come around to a more thoughtful manner and say something like, "But your organization has done a good job for many years. Maybe this is a one-time incident. What I want to do is get it all squared away and fix this problem so it doesn't happen again."

The rule of thumb is to exhibit the behavior you want the customer to adopt in his dealings with you. If he observes you doing your best to remain thoughtful and resolve the problem, in all probability he will come around.

Let go of anger. Holding on to feelings of disappointment, rage, and resentment can cause bitterness and block your efforts to relate to the customer.

Try forgiving and forgetting as a way of putting anger away. Move in a direction that will build the relationship and help you maintain your self-respect.

Think positive outcomes. When you are really hurting, focus on what you will gain by not surrendering to anger. Ask yourself the question, "How will we both benefit if I act out my anger on the customer?" The answer will become obvious. "Neither of us will."

By focusing on the gain, you place a priority on the positive outcomes you see at the end of the rainbow. If you see the pot of gold as worth it, then you will be more inclined to endure the short-term discomfort.

Make a deal with yourself. Even though your emotional muscles may be tired, you are really in control. Your ability to control how you react will give you a higher sense of self-regard and personal power. Make a deal with yourself to resist getting hooked on anger.

SIGNS OF INDIFFERENCE

Sometimes we hear what the customer is saying, but immediately file it away in the "Unimportant—To Be Ignored" folder. What we're saying, in effect, is, "Don't confuse me with the facts: I've already got my mind made up."

An attitude of indifference reflects your own belief that you have an inexhaustible fund of knowledge to which the customer can add little or nothing. This attitude says to the customer:

"YOUR THOUGHTS AND OPINIONS ARE INTERESTING,
BUT WHAT I'VE GOT TO SAY
WILL SET YOU FREE."

When you have the "resident expert" approach to working with the customer, you set yourself up as the answer person. You place so much importance on the value of what you have to say that you are completely indifferent to what's on the customer's mind.

Overcoming Indifference

Remain influenceable. Respond to the customer from the neck up and from the neck down: Use your heart as well as your head. Be open to the facts, data, and details the customer can give you, but also be responsive to the way he feels.

Treat the customer seriously. Pay attention to the symptoms before you go after the cause. Treat his concerns with respect and you may find that the problem goes away by itself. But if you remain indifferent, the problem will never get better.

Don't have all the answers. Having all the answers is the surest sign that you believe yourself to be the resident expert. By admitting you *don't* have all the answers, you could earn the customer's trust—and that's money in your bank account.

SIGNS OF IMPATIENCE

Do you ever find yourself thinking these kinds of thoughts while the customer's talking?

"Why do I have to sit here and hear her out? I already know what she needs."

"I can't wait for him to stop talking, so he can hear what I have to say."

By prematurely building your reply, you block your ability to hear the customer's point of view. In turn, your response may not take the real issue into account. This is a sure sign of *impatience*.

Overcoming Impatience

Don't jump the gun. When you become overeager, you start paying too much attention to what *you* want to say. You miss what you should be hearing. If your impatience cuts off the customer, your conclusions are based on an incomplete understanding of his total concern.

Stay open to new data. What the customer tells you today is vital to your understanding of the current situation and problem. Your prior knowledge may now be completely out of date or irrelevant. Remain open, influenceable, and ready to shape your response to take the customer's point of view into account.

Manage your enthusiasm. Harness your enthusiasm so as not to overwhelm the customer with your energy. Let the customer express himself freely and completely—*then* use your enthusiasm to express your belief in your solution. By controlling your impatience, you show greater confidence in yourself and in what you're selling. You put your energy to work understanding the customer rather than overwhelming him.

SIGNS OF PREOCCUPATION

In addition to Anger, Indifference, and Impatience, there is a fourth sign of self-centeredness—Preoccupation. We have many reasons for being preoccupied. Perhaps you're still dwelling on the results of your previous sales call. Or you're worried about your next appointment. If this is the case, you may be suffering from brain drift: Your mind wanders while the customer is talking.

Overcoming Preoccupation

Stay alert. Talk yourself into concentrating. If you find yourself mentally critiquing the customer's language, manners, or style, you know you're getting off the track.

Jolt yourself back to the present. Think to yourself: What's the customer really trying to tell me? If you don't understand what the customer is saying, ask for clarification.

Write it down. If you feel the urge to daydream, connect your brain to a pencil. Ask the customer for permission to take notes while he's talking. The very act of taking notes will keep you squarely focused on what the customer is saying.

Begin the night before. If you really want to combat brain drift, you have to begin the night before. Your life-style will affect the quality of your work. Mental alertness is impossible if you're fighting off the effects of alcohol fatigue or a late night on the town. Get the rest you need. Don't let alcohol siphon off your energy. You can't keep your brain in gear when your guts are rumbling.

When you see telltale signs of Anger, Indifference, Impatience, and Preoccupation in your reactions to the customer, ask yourself how you can *stop looking out for Number One.*

The best way is by choosing the behaviors that will lead to favorable outcomes for you and your customers. It's up to you to decide whether you are going to employ a self-centered reaction or an other-centered response to the customer's words. If you choose an other-centered response, you truly put the customer's interests above your own.

I am reminded of one of my favorite movies, *Miracle on 34th Street,* in which a department-store Santa Claus hired by Macy's listens attentively to each child's wishes. But Santa defies his employer by telling one child's mother where she can find his gift in *another* store!

His honesty and truthfulness make Macy's Santa Claus so popular that the management can't fire him—he is drawing in customers in *record* numbers!

In *Miracle on 34th Street,* integrity, truthfulness, and caring turn a department-store Santa Claus into a *real* Santa Claus, true to the spirit of giving.

Listening is an act of giving.

When you *listen* to the customer and try to understand his problems, you're saying, "Right now, your thoughts are more important to me than my very own."

That's a powerful message.

To my way of thinking, the highest level of professionalism in sales is served by having the lowest ego involvement.

To understand what's happening—and to *make* things happen—you have to get out of your own and into the other person's skin. You will then be ready to handle any objection or any resistance that comes from the customer. You will be prepared for the Third Strategy for Positioning:

INVEST IN THE RELATIONSHIP

5

The Third Strategy for Positioning:
Invest in the Relationship

Some salespeople specialize in hip-pocket replies when they encounter negative customer reactions. Here's one of my favorites.

A salesman I know was trying to remedy an account that had been nothing but trouble. But the buyer he met with was not exactly encouraging:

> "Randy, you're a very nice guy to come in here and try to patch this thing up, but you're wasting your time. If your president were here, I'd give him a piece of my mind. Your organization screwed us up, and we're not going to take another chance with you guys because you don't deserve it."

That's when Randy launched into what I call "The War Reply."

"Pat," he said, "what you said to me now reminds me of what happened forty-five years ago when we went to war. Who were our two biggest adversaries in the Second World War?"

"Germany and Japan," Pat replied, puzzled.

"You're right, Pat, Germany and Japan. And today, Pat, who are our biggest allies?"

"Germany and Japan."

"That's right!" said Randy. "That's exactly my point! America was big enough to forgive, Pat. Are *you*?"

Zaaaaaap!

A direct hit!

But Randy isn't the only salesperson to use hip-pocket zingers like that.

I used to memorize them, just so I'd have a snappy answer any time a buyer sneaked up on me with an objection.

Here's another one:

"Well, Tom, if you can *buy* it from *someone else* for less, then that's probably what it's worth! After all, you usually *get* what you pay for."

Or how about this winner—when the buyer confronted me with, "I'm not sure I want to change." This is what I would say:

"I think you'd agree that the only time we change is when we want to better an existing situation and when we know it's better to change. And when it's better to change, then the sooner we change, the better—right, Tom?"

Or if the customer was angry at me for a late shipment or poor quality:

"You may be mad at me now, Tom. But you're not mad at money, are you? And I'm talking about making you *real money!*"

I was always proud of myself when I got off a shot like that because I knew I had *scored,* I had *fixed* him, I had hit him so hard he'd be down for the count and if he was lucky enough to get off the mat, I'd be ready for another swipe.

My message to the buyer was:

I CAN HIT ANY PITCH YOU THROW AT ME!

From my exterior, though, you wouldn't guess that was my attitude. On the outside, I was friendly, courteous, eager to please. But underneath all that, there was anger, indifference, impatience, and *preoccupation with my own concerns.* Worst of all, I felt contempt for what the buyer was trying to tell me because I didn't attach much seriousness to what he was saying.

I wasn't trying to understand. I was trying to *score.*

And as a result, I came off sounding more like a door-to-door, fast-talking con artist than a sales professional.

I've discovered that a lot of salespeople rely on canned answers as a protective device.

Whenever the customer raises an objection, we feel like the target—whether we are or not.

Yet meeting customer resistance is all part of selling. We face it every day.

A publisher's rep is likely to hear, "I don't have space for your titles—I'm overstocked as it is."

An area sales representative for a beverage company is told by her distributor, "Your brand just isn't moving as well as my other labels."

Sitting at the kitchen table in a client's home, a financial counselor is told, "We really can't decide without talking to my brother-in-law—he's an investment broker."

A yacht broker is ready to close the sale when she gets a call from the prospective buyer. "Norma, I've reconsidered. It's a luxury item we just can't afford right now."

At the moment when a friendly merger is about to go through, the president of an industrial company is visited by legal counsel for the other firm: "I'm sorry," he's told, "my client just can't agree to these terms."

Objections that first seem "negative"—the kind that prevent sales—are not necessarily a complete rejection of you or your recommended solution. These reactions could mean that the customer needs more information, wants assurance, or is nervous about making a buying decision. Objections can also stem from a totally unrelated problem such as the pressure of work, frequent and unwanted interruptions, a personal difficulty, or even the unprofessional and irritating behavior of the salesperson who called on the customer before you walked in the door. Any kind of temporary frustration may wind up on your shoulders in the form of an objection.

Not long ago, at the request of one of my clients, I accompanied a software consultant, Darrel Carpenter, on a sales call to a systems analyst for a large northeastern insurance company. It was a closing call.

From the moment we walked in the office, I could tell that everything was going well between Darrel and his client. Ann Maxwell, the systems analyst, was obviously impressed with Darrel—they had a good working relationship—and all signs were favorable for concluding an agreement.

After we'd been there a few minutes, however, Ann said, "Darrel, I have to ask you something that worries me. This system tests out well. But my people would like to have some assurances that we can get all the necessary service support in the future."

I glanced at Darrel. He wasn't prepared for this, and I could see by the expression on his face that he was shocked.

"I don't understand," he said, reflecting a degree of irritation. "I thought I did a complete job of describing our service plan. Is there something I didn't make clear?" He paused—not really waiting for an answer. Then he tried the clincher: "Why would I try to sell you a system that we couldn't back up?"

From that moment on, the sales call went downhill. Ann became defensive and her tone became challenging. Darrel became progressively more confrontational—though he tried to hide his feelings behind a solid wall of arguments.

The meeting concluded early—and without a sale. Afterward, we talked about it.

"I can't understand what happened!" Darrel fumed. "Where did she get the idea that we couldn't back our product? She must have talked to someone who gave us a bad recommendation."

I could see that Darrel was about to go into a "blaming" routine, and I patiently waited him out before we began to talk about it.

After some discussion, it became clear that Darrel had jumped to the conclusion that Ann was accusing him. He hadn't given her a chance to tell him what was on her mind. He had simply overreacted.

Like many salespeople, Darrel believed that he had to have an instant answer to every objection.

He was like me in the days of my hip-pocket ditties—guilty as charged.

In the process model I'm about to share with you, you'll notice there are no pat phrases. Our focus will be not on an answer but on a straight-talking process. I won't tell you exactly what to say and how to say it, but I'll provide some examples of the four steps that work for thousands of sales professionals.

The fact is, if you're building your reply—or you already have one in your briefcase—then you're not *listening* to the buyer. And when you don't listen, you can't respond in a responsible, caring manner.

THE *PROCESS* IS THE SOLUTION!

The whole purpose of the process, which I call LAER, is to make you alert to the fact that you're dealing with a *real* person with *real* problems. And when you're doing that, the first thing you have to do is throw away those canned replies.

The beauty of the process of LAER is that it looks out for the customer's interests as well as your own. It creates a bond between you and the customer, while at the same time responding to his objections.

A bond between two people is a union for mutual benefit. The process of bonding takes place when you understand the customer's point of view and work toward a mutually beneficial outcome. You demonstrate your interest, support, and understanding—and work toward a resolution.

COMMUNICATING IS MEETING PEOPLE HALFWAY.
LAER IS GOING A LITTLE BIT FURTHER.

When you picture LAER in your mind, think of each step—Listen, Acknowledge, Explore, Respond—as being interconnected by a network of customer-centered interactions:

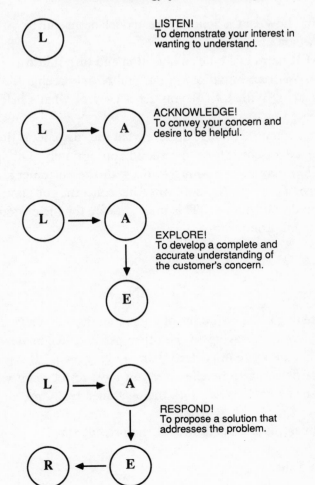

LISTEN!
To demonstrate your interest in
wanting to understand.

ACKNOWLEDGE!
To convey your concern and
desire to be helpful.

EXPLORE!
To develop a complete and
accurate understanding of
the customer's concern.

RESPOND!
To propose a solution that
addresses the problem.

Now, how can a four-square model be useful to you as a salesperson?

LAER helps you take an objection and turn it into an opportunity. With an initial objection, you're only seeing the tip of the iceberg. With LAER you get a view of what's below the surface.

What you need to do is explore what the customer is thinking so you can discover how to respond appropriately. The spoken objection may have nothing to do with the customer's actual concern. To get to the bottom of his concern, you have to be open and nondefensive. This makes it safe for the customer to express his true feelings.

LISTEN

Listening is the beginning of understanding. When you listen closely, you are saying to the other person, "Right now your thoughts are more important than my very own." But for that kind of listening to be effective, you have to focus on what is really being said. What does the customer really mean?

"Our needs are being met at the present time."

Could mean:

"I'm having a busy day and can't take time to listen to your proposal right now."

"Your competitor is a good friend and I can't let him down."

"We have some other needs—but I'm not even considering them at the moment."

Hear the customer out. Don't become defensive about yourself or your company. If you become oversensitive to one portion of the customer's concern, you won't hear the entire message. Don't miss the payoff.

It's been my experience that the customer who feels listened to and understood is more likely to listen in return and to be open to changing his mind. Warm and attentive listening may be all you need to defuse the objection and move the transaction along.

And now that you've listened . . . *take credit for it* in the next step of the process, acknowledging.

ACKNOWLEDGE

Acknowledging prevents a tug of war between you and the customer. When you're acknowledging, actions speak as loudly as words. A simple nod of the head, good eye-contact, leaning forward in your seat, a concerned facial expression—these are signs of interest.

If you're really paying attention, your body language will express what you feel—attentiveness, concern, interest, or surprise.

The verbal acknowledgment allows you to take credit for listening. You can do that with words such as:

"I share your concern."

"I understand."

"Thank you for sharing that with me."

"That makes sense."

"I hear what you are saying."

"I am not discounting your concern."

"I am interested in helping."

The acknowledgment has to be sincere—not a syrupy ploy that patronizes the customer. Otherwise the customer will *see through* your saccharin attempts to sweeten him up.

In discussing the value of the acknowledgment with sales colleagues, I've concluded that the acknowledgment has a tranquilizing effect. It helps you circumvent arguments and elicits restraint from the customer. When you acknowledge the customer's words, he will feel safe in communicating his full range of concerns.

REMEMBER, A WAR NOT WAGED IS A WAR WON.

When you acknowledge a customer's concerns by repeating them in your own words, a very subtle change occurs. *You take possession of those concerns.*

The concerns become a part of you. By voicing the customer's point of view for a moment, you cross the line. You stand on his side and say to yourself and to him, "So this is the way it is."

Acknowledging has enormous payoffs. You get a chance to collect your thoughts. You find out how strong his feelings are. And you create the momentum to flow directly into the next step of the bonding process, the "explore" phase.

EXPLORE

When you explore, you're trying to understand the specific issues underlying the customer's resistance. You've just had a first glimpse of the objection. Now you're going for the whole picture—to find out where that objection comes from and what it really means.

- Does the customer need more information?
- Do you need to tell him more about your organization?
- Is there a hidden objection?
- Are you making yourself clearly understood?
- How intense is his resistance?
- Are you talking about the same things?

In the exploring step, you ask the customer for help in understanding his problem. This can be done either by asking helpful questions or by making a statement in which you attempt to restate and verify what the customer has said.

Exploring questions are *helping* questions. Here are a few examples of what would be considered exploring:

"Ann, I need your help to comprehend fully . . ."

"Could you give me some additional information about . . ."

"Thank you for sharing your concern. What you are saying is . . ."

"Is my understanding complete and accurate?"

Don't let my choice of words in this example distract you from the purpose of the process. There are lots of different directions in which you can go. The key to finding the real objection is to keep the process active. As you explore, you must listen to the feedback and acknowledge it.

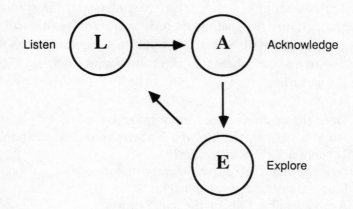

You may have to acknowledge and explore several times to get to the root of the problem. But as you do, you are bonding more closely to the customer because you are enlisting his support. In fact, throughout the process, I frequently say to the customer, "I'd like to understand . . . but I need your help. Am I dealing with your real concern?"

RESPOND

When you have Listened, Acknowledged, and Explored, you are ready for the final step in the bonding process. You are ready to Respond.

The response is the logical conclusion to the interplay of the preceding steps.

In responding, you provide an answer to the customer's objection in the form of a recommendation, an alternative, a solution statement, or a suggestion for a next step. Your response is designed to bring the LAER process to a close, so that you can proceed to the next appropriate activity in the sales call.

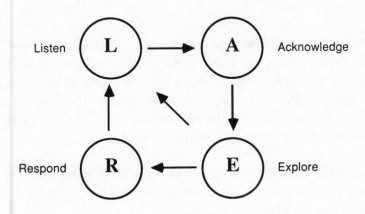

In the case of the price objection, your response could be:

"You're right, John, you could get it for a lower price. However, I feel that the value of our program and the service I'll provide are more important assets than a lower price."

If a customer objects to poor service or a performance deficiency, you might respond in detail:

"Karen, I'm glad we reviewed some of the problems you've been having. I'd like to specify some of the corrective action steps that we plan to take. Our goal is to solve these problems and prevent them from recurring."

Or, if a customer says he wants to talk it over with his personal or professional associates:

> "Tom, that makes a lot of good business sense. By the same token, based upon what I've shown you so far, do you feel positive enough about this program to recommend it to your associates?"

By having LAER at your command, you are always in position. You are equipped with a strategy that lets you respond to any objection at any time during a sales transaction. When you are open to the customer's concerns, you will *welcome* his objections; they give you the opportunity to move the transaction forward rather than shutting it down.

In using LAER, remember that exploring is not probing. There's one certain way to make sure you never resort to a probe. *Use the Columbo method!*

Slouching around in his trench coat as "Detective Columbo," Peter Falk used the finest method known to humankind for getting help from another person—he *asked* for it.

> "Say, I'm a—a little confused. Maybe you can help me out. I thought you said the guy drowned. But see, he had this little hole in his chest. And I was wondering . . ."

Columbo got the kind of help from witnesses that no inspector, D.A., or expert prosecutor could ever obtain. And he did it *without* a white light and rubber hose.

A lot of salespeople swear by *Gotcha!* questions—the kinds of questions preferred by public prosecutors and litigious trial lawyers.

But there's a flaw in that.

When you try to get information from a buyer with *Gotcha!* questions, you're stacking the deck—setting the person up to agree with your position.

Gotcha! tactics can take many forms.

There's the *leading statement:*

"Don't you agree that we give outstanding service?"

"Do you mean that you would actually settle for inferior quality?"

"Aren't reducing costs and saving money important to you?"

"Isn't it true that we're a reliable supplier?"

There's the *cross-examination:*

"Why has timing suddenly become an issue?"

"Are you sure you followed our instructions?"

"What, exactly, do you expect me to do about what's happened?"

And the *punitive probe:*

"Are you suggesting that my company does not have the ability to perform?"

"Why do you insist on installing the system this way?"

"You don't think we can deliver what we promise?"

Gotcha! tactics may indeed get the customer where he hurts, but these tactics won't get *you* anywhere. If you expect any customer to stay with you for the long haul, you'd better *listen* to that person and *take him seriously.* You can't ask him to confide in you and then reward his confidence with a series of punishing questions. He'll freeze up. He'll take his business elsewhere.

The fact is, if you want a long-term relationship, you have to be able to take the bad with the good—you have to deal with the devastating objection on the front end, which will result in the buy-in to your program on the back end. And that means you have to *explore* to find out what's wrong—even though you might turn up a few things you prefer not to find. You're going to have to deal with them sooner or later.

Forget about yourself during the process.

Find out what's troubling the buyer.

And take his objection *seriously.*

Some time ago, a neighbor of mine, Frankie "Fats" Gallagher, held a huge clambake for everyone on the street.

Frankie had a whole bucketful of clams. But during a moment of libation and merriment, he accidentally crashed his bulky frame into the clam bucket.

Now, everyone knows that clams go into shock if they get a sudden jolt. True to their name and reputation, they "clam up"—and after that, they're impossible to open.

Frankie tried to pry a few open, but failed miserably. Finally, in desperation, he got out his trusty hammer and chisel and went to work.

Well, he succeeded in opening the clams, but he destroyed them in the process. And my friends and I spent the rest of the evening removing shell fragments from between our teeth before we could consume those tender morsels.

Probing is the *hammer-and-chisel* approach to selling. You may get the customer to open up, but you destroy the relationship in the process. It's *instant gratification* behavior instead of *long-term investment* behavior.

With LAER you don't *have* to have hip-pocket answers,

because you have the *process* to help you respond. If you follow the steps—Listen, Acknowledge, and Explore—the Response will be provided as much by the buyer as it is by you.

Although LAER is a *contingency* strategy for handling objections and is not intended for making a presentation, there are two occasions when you might use this strategy for getting an order. First, if you're calling on an already established account, and you know the buyer has a *complaint* or a *problem,* then use LAER. Secondly, if you're a trouble shooter or claims adjuster, remember this could be a primary strategy for you.

All four steps of LAER are directed toward a single goal—to help *you* understand and respond.

As Positional Selling strategies have been utilized by a growing number of companies, it has been interesting to hear how LAER has been used not only as an objection-handling process but also as a means of *improving relationships* inside an organization. When someone airs an objection or voices a grievance, he wants to be heard. And LAER is a model that reduces conflict and normalizes the situation because no one can keep arguing with someone who is really and truly trying to understand and be helpful.

I once worked as a part-time bartender at Cunningham's Bar & Grill on Long Island when I was going through college. And that's where I came to understand the meaning of a simple term for listening: it's called *Bartending the Buyer.*

Cunningham's was the local watering hole where the off-duty firemen and cops used to wet their whistles. And I quickly observed that if Jack Carew shut his mouth and *listened* to them, he got bigger tips than if he talked about himself. Learning *when to keep my mouth shut* and attentively listen to their exciting exploits turned out to be a valuable lesson in economics.

Bartending the buyer by using LAER is the best strategy I know for handling an objection that's emotionally loaded.

On numerous occasions I've handled emotional objections from buyers who were ready to throw me out the door. And I know that LAER works—because, above all, the buyer wants to be *heard.* And LAER is the strategy that *forces you to listen* without contaminating the message you receive. Your own self-interest doesn't stand in the way.

But there are also times when a person simply can't take any more—and LAER can tell you *that,* too. We've all seen what happens in late afternoon, between 3:00 and 4:30, when the anxiety level is at its highest. All the stress is there. The day has caught up with the customer. As a rule, late afternoon is when you're most likely to get a knuckle sandwich. The customer is more volatile than he is in the morning when he's refreshed, when his mind is clear, and when he's not confused and over-loaded.

In Saudi Arabia I've heard people refer to a quality called "fullness." The Saudis say, "Once in a while a person becomes *full.* He's full of all the distractions, full of all the pressure, full of his wife, full of his kids, full of *life.* And anything you try to pour in on top of him only upsets him because he's *full.* You may have a *great idea* but he's not ready for it yet."

There have been times when I called on a customer with an idea that I thought was destined to change his life—and found he was reluctant to get into the details. He wanted to delay the discussion because he was just *up to his neck.* That's fullness. And when a buyer is full, you don't want to pack anything in on top of it, because he won't be able to handle it—and *you'll* become a target for his frustrations.

For the sales professional, LAER is a powerful strategy. It can overcome anger, indifference, impatience, and preoccupation. When you Listen, Acknowledge, and Explore before you Respond, you focus squarely on the customer's Operating Reality. Every objection then becomes an opportunity to know the customer better—and to establish your own credentials as a problem-solver.

Instead of *reacting* to the buyer with a memorized, smart-aleck retort that leads to a no-win engagement, you let the person know, "I'm paying attention to what you're saying. And I want to know more about what it is we're dealing with, so I can be helpful."

By creating a climate of understanding and cooperation, you can turn a no-win shooting match into a win-win relationship.

You're not just handling an objection. You're creating a lasting and permanent bond.

You're investing in the relationship.

6

The Fourth Strategy for Positioning:
Bring Your Energy to the Customer

Here's what a buyer usually does about fifteen minutes before
I show up for a sales presentation:

First, he has a short period of Transcendental Meditation to
clear his mind of all the confusion, stress, and preoccupation
that he's had during the day. Then he says to his secretary,
"Mary, Jack Carew is coming in to make a presentation and I'd
like two sharpened pencils and a lined yellow pad so I can make
notes of everything that Mr. Carew has to say. And have a nice
cup of coffee for him so that when he gets here, we let him know
that we're looking out for him."

And when I walk in the door, the buyer says, "Jack, I'm
anxiously looking forward to what you have to say today."

Do you know any buyers like that?
Neither do I!
You usually walk in while the buyer's in the middle of a
phone conversation. And as you come in the room, he's saying,
"All right, Martin . . . Yes! . . . Yes, *please take care of it!*

... I *know* it's a horrible mess, but we've got to get rolling again because we've got a *job that ships in three days.* Yeh . . . yeh—No, I can't go to lunch with you guys. I've got a guy coming in today. . . . I've got to see him in a few minutes. . . . Yes, I promise to get back to you. . . . Yeh, fine, very good, very good—

"Oh, hi, Jack, how ya doing—what's up?"

Is that more like it?

Well, if it is, then you know your work's cut out for you from the instant you come in the door. Somehow, you have to *clear away* all those distractions from the customer's mind. You also have to eliminate distractions from your own mind, because *it's what's important to the customer that counts.*

In other words, you have to make Positive Contact.

In making Positive Contact, it's absolutely essential that you bring your energy to the customer. You have to get into the customer's Operating Reality immediately and stay there.

It means that you say to yourself:

"While I am here with the customer, I am not engaged in any other activity."

Think about that. This means that it is essential for you to clear your mind of unrelated mental preoccupation and pay attention to what's important to the customer. His children, his hobbies, his weekend, and his special interests. Not yours, but his.

This requires that you abandon your self-interest long enough to establish and maintain warm and enthusiastic contact with the customer. Remember the rule I mentioned?

THE CUSTOMER WILL FIND
SOMETHING WRONG WITH WHAT YOU ARE SELLING
IF HE FINDS SOMETHING WRONG WITH YOU.

Whether or not salespeople become magnets for objections is directly related to how they establish contact at the outset of the transaction. If you get off to a shaky start, the customer will look for things he doesn't like, rather than the things he does like, about what you represent. The quality of the sales call will deteriorate rapidly. If you get off to a bad start, the customer will mentally "punch your ticket" and say, "Next!"

To get started on the right foot, remember Positive Contact! Positive Contact is the opening step in *any* sales transaction, whether you're making a needs-identification sales call or presenting a product or service. How you establish Positive Contact ultimately determines the effectiveness of all the other strategies of Positional Selling.

There are three elements that win the buyer's attention and keep his attention throughout the sales call. These elements are Attitude, Energy, and Appearance.

ATTITUDE

Attitudes are built and maintained by the messages we send ourselves. Tell yourself, "My time is valuable. I want this sales call to be successful. I am competent, prepared, and ready to make an outstanding contribution. I see myself as being helpful and capable of bringing value to the customer."

These attitudes will be translated into actions that will create and build momentum at the outset of the sales call.

Shake off the energy-draining effects of shock, denial, and blaming that could be caused by the punishing impact of rejection experienced on a previous sales call. Move from acceptance into renewal by anticipating the positive outcomes that are possible on this sales call.

For some salespeople, winter is never over. They only see the dark side. Chronically depressed salespeople spend more time worrying about what will go wrong than concentrating on what can go right. These are the kind of salespeople who feel good by feeling bad.

They see themselves as unwelcome guests, with the customer as an adversary waiting to pounce on them. If this is the way you view yourself, count on acting out these perceptions. It will be very difficult to feel one way and act another way.

What do you *think* of the buyer? What's really going on in your head before the sales call? Are you determined to do the *best you can* for this person? And are you trying to find *the very best in him or her?*

ENERGY

The electricity that makes your life worthwhile is sparked by the excitement and stimulation that's created when you meet people, deal with people, and work with people. And if you can't get excited about what you're selling, how can anyone else?

Some salespeople make sales calls as if they were spending their first day in a nudist camp. They fig-leaf it! Their very presence, tone of voice, posture, and movement is evidence of insecurity, hesitancy, and uncertainty. They are so frozen with fright that they are incapable of making any Positive Contact.

- What happens in those first two to sixty seconds you're face to face with the buyer?
- How do you act when you are dealing with established accounts?
- Do those relationships become stale?
- Do you always bring your energy to the customer?

Find your speed and be natural. You determine the tempo of the transaction. From the moment you meet the customer, you begin to determine the outcome. You are everything that you feel, believe, and do.

One of the most energetic sales professionals I've had the privilege of knowing is my colleague Andy Sloan. Working with Andy is like being on the winning team in the closing minutes of a basketball game. Andy *generates* energy by running faster, playing harder and having more fun than anyone else on the court. That energy gets through to *my* team and it gets through to *his* customers. When Andy has a clear shot, he doesn't miss—because he's got *everyone* cheering for him.

If you're a prospect of Andy's, and you're in the office by nine o'clock, you'll get a call at 9:01. And I guarantee it's a call you won't forget!

APPEARANCE

People attach meanings to you without really thinking about it. That's why it's essential to pay close attention to every aspect of your appearance. You need to convey seriousness and professionalism.

A colleague of mine, Professor Peter Barth of Brazil, in comparing doing business in Rio de Janeiro and São Paulo, once told me that the only time you wear a tie in Rio is when you are married, when you are buried, and when you're really serious about getting a bank loan.

What you wear depends on who you are, where you are, and whom you're seeing. Nevertheless, there are two rules that hold true in sales: *Always* look neat, clean, and well-groomed; *always* look rested, nonstressed, and attentive.

In the service, there's an old saying: When in doubt, salute! In selling, the saying goes like this: When in doubt, dress up!

It shows respect—and the customer will appreciate you for being held in high regard.

Don't forget that the night before can ruin your appearance the day after. When you're coping with the negative effects of alcohol fatigue and overeating, your appearance suffers. Glassy eyes, bad breath, and body odor send the message, "I don't care enough to be my very best."

Your Attitude, Energy, and Appearance, like the first bars in a melody or song, *hook* the buyer, so you have his attention.

Of course, people are *born* with hooks. They're called *names*.

There are many reasons to use the customer's name at every appropriate opportunity. People like being called by their names. It's personal, it's intimate, and it gets you started on the right foot.

Then there's a very practical reason. The more you use someone else's name, the more likely you are to remember that person by name.

If you want to remember people's names, try these approaches. They work:

1. Say to yourself at the first moment of your first encounter: "There is no business more important to me right now than learning and remembering this person's name."
2. Repeat that name: "How are you, Ed?" or "Delighted finally to meet you, Martha." This lets you hear the name a second time.
3. Then think of a positive quality you see in that person that begins with the same letter as the first name. For example, Enthusiastic Ed or Efficient Ed or Motivated Martha or Marvelous Martha. By connecting a positive quality with the name, you paint a *positive word picture* of that person. Use that picture to help you recall the name.
4. Use the customer's name during the transaction to generate an appropriate level of intimacy. You will create a

feeling of teamwork and break through the barrier of the customer's preoccupations.

5. At the first opportunity, write down the full name. Even if you have exchanged business cards with the customer, *write* his name as well as look at it. The act of connecting your brain to the name by way of a pencil captures an indelible image that will remain in your mind.

There are six action steps for bringing your energy to the customer:

1. GET OUT OF THE ASSEMBLY AREA!

A good friend of mine who was operating a sales organization in the Cleveland area looked as if he had all the credentials in the world to do a great job. He had a solid sales background, an advanced degree, and he knew all the management methods for scientifically leading a sales team.

But he failed miserably. The sales organization let him continue for approximately two years and then let him go.

Not too long after he was relieved of duty, I happened to be talking with one of his colleagues and I asked the question:

"Whatever happened to Gary? He had everything going for him! Why did he fail?"

And his colleague said, "Jack, for this reason: *He never got out of the Assembly Area.*"

In the military, the Assembly Area is where you prepare for an assault. That's where you do your organization work and get mentally and physically prepared for engagement.

So I knew what happened. Gary spent so much time *preparing* and *contemplating* action that he never went out and made contact with the customer.

He sat back and talked a good game, but he never executed.

He became so obsessed with planning and preparing that he neglected to seek engagement.

Strategy is important. But as one military leader put it, "To hell with long-range plans. We've got to take the hill now!"

So this is your first and most important step toward bringing your energy to the customer:

GET OUT OF THE ASSEMBLY AREA! TAKE THE HILL
NOW!

2. EARN POSITION

Some salespeople are fortunate enough to have position *provided to them* by virtue of what they're selling. The corporate name attached to their product or the uniqueness of what they have to offer gives them favored placement in the marketplace.

When position is *provided,* a salesperson can sometimes be successful in spite of himself. For example, when a customer is desperate for a product, providing that product is like selling a life preserver to a drowning man. Because the company is so well known and the product so highly regarded, salespeople with *provided position* can stumble their way through a call and still get the deal. The *intensity of the buyer's need* turns the tables in the salesperson's favor and lets him off the hook.

But the real sales heroes are those who *earn position.* For salespeople with unknown company brands, products, or services—or for salespeople who are out there representing their own companies—it's a matter of constantly doing missionary work. You have to establish new markets, educate accounts, and sell products and services that no one knows anything about. Salespeople who *earn position* really have to work hard because they must create an awareness that wasn't previously there.

The transformation that has occurred in banking services is a dramatic example of how a whole industry can change from *provided position* to *earned position*.

Today, there's a great deal of competitive activity in banking because so many institutions are now selling financial services. Your friendly banker-on-the-corner sitting securely behind a mahogany desk in a fifty-three-piece suit—the guy you used to approach hat in hand for a line of credit—is a thing of the past.

Typically, *you* were the one who went to see the banker, and he exercised all the power and influence. You waited by the gate outside his little area, and when you came in, you always referred to him as "Mister." He got information from you that was very sensitive and he handled the documents that you were supposed to sign. The banker was all-powerful.

But today, the banker's dominant position is not so secure. A lot of people are after his business, and any financial institution that wants to remain competitive has to *get out of the Assembly Area* and engage the client. It's imperative for today's banker to emerge from behind the mahogany desk and bring his energy to the customer.

3. FEEL GOOD ABOUT THE PEOPLE YOU'RE CALLING ON

One of the best salespeople I've ever known is a man named Chuck Lea in Cincinnati, Ohio.

Before he goes inside a building to call on a buyer, Chuck Lea reaches out his arms and says, "I love everyone inside. They're doing their very best. Besides, God did not make shoddy goods!"

For Chuck Lea the gesture is more than symbolic. When he's with the customer he *acts out* these positive feelings. His warm manner and his sincere smile actually *change the day* for everyone he sees. He's hopeful, he's positive, and he goes into each call with a sense of anticipation and expectancy that is *communicated to the people he calls on.*

The fact is, if your heart is in the right place, that will carry the rest of your body.

4. TOUCH EVERYONE

When you bring your energy to the customer, you have to remember that you're not just calling on one buyer in a vacuum.

THE BUYER IS EVERYONE.

Some salespeople do a good job of selling the person who makes the buying decision, but they leave a trail of dead bodies along the way.

You have to touch all bases! You don't have the luxury of resting with one advocate who loves you while you create numerous adversaries who would be happy to see you go. You have to be able to reach into the organization and get people to rally around you.

A salesperson who brings his energy to everyone will get people *wanting him to be successful.* If your relationship with the customer's support people begins to deteriorate, you lose position. Those support people are the ones who make what you sell work.

Take time out for the "small people" in the company—people who have minor jobs, who don't get paid very much, who are not considered important or treated as important.

Someone who's over in a corner someplace punching a word processor may surprise you. That's the person who, one day, discovers a mistake in your invoice and says, "Hey, Jack, I found something. Maybe you want to take care of it? Because I need to show it to someone—and I know it isn't right."

You know what happens? That person keeps negative traffic out of the sight and consciousness of other people in his organization. That's the person who covers for you and helps you straighten things out before bad news gets to his boss.

But if the people don't like you, they'll look for your slip-up. And when they find it, they'll run to their boss and say, "Listen, this guy did a lousy job again. *And here's proof!*"

In every operation, there are a lot of people who are treated like workers. They do a day's work and get a day's pay.

Find the toughest guy and say, "How are you, Tommy?"

No reply.

The next time. "How are you doing, Tommy?"

When the coffee wagon comes around, buy him a donut and a cup of coffee.

If you do that often enough, Tommy gets warmer. Finally, one day, he says to you, "Look, a guy was out here the other day—one of your competitors . . ."

In a plant I used to visit, I had two good friends, Mario Biancalana and Chester Grabowski. I called them The Irish Combination.

If my company shipped defective goods, they *never* reported it to the purchasing agent. They would take me aside: "Hey, Jack, come back here. You've got to do something about this. It's the third time. Now, look, we didn't say anything, but if they find us out here with this stuff, we're in a jam."

Furthermore, I *always* knew about my competitors nosing around. I used to get complete reports. Mario or Chet would come up to me and say, "Consolidated was over here last week nosing around. But don't worry. We won't let them in."

That kind of loyalty saved me on many occasions.

Sometimes your advocate is pressed to reevaluate the performance of existing suppliers. Some trailblazer in his company will eventually say to him, "I want to audit all vendor relationships." (Trailblazers are always brought in to shake the tree.)

If you have people on your side, everyone will find a way to make *you* look good—and put your competitor in a lesser light.

What they're really saying is that they want you to be there. In addition to price, service, quality, and delivery, *you* make the difference.

5. USE ALL YOUR ASSETS

I used to work for a boss named Charlie Leonard who was a valuable teacher because he never let me off the hook.

His motto was: "What will it take—within reason—to get the business?"

Whatever it took—that's what we had to do. Would it help if he made a sales call with me? Could he bring in the production people to help me out? What did I need?

"Jack," he'd say, "what will it take to make this guy say yes?"

Charlie was very clear about this. I would hem and haw and say, "Well, we've got a problem about this and that."

And he'd say, "All right, now let's look at this problem. *In your estimation,* what will it take to *write business* and *build a relationship* with this person?"

This kind of support made me look at myself and say, "Why am I making excuses?"

Because what Charlie was telling me was this: "There is no asset in this organization that's not available to you to help you sell."

He cut off my escape routes. He kicked the crutches out from under me and made me stand on my own two feet.

I was fortunate to have Charlie Leonard at that point in my career. A lot of salespeople have assets they don't use—and often, the sales manager *doesn't tell them what those assets are.*

If the only people you see as your assets are the customers, you're shortchanging yourself. When you bring your energy to the customer, you're not just bringing *yourself* to the transaction. You're bringing the people and the unique capabilities of your organization, as well. But you have to be able to *manage* those assets in order to succeed.

6. SHARE YOUR EXCITEMENT

We all need positive stress to challenge and stimulate us. Convert this stress into energy that you bring to the customer. Energy is infectious. It charges the atmosphere. It creates results. A person who is prepared shows his preparedness. A person who is confident brings confidence into the room. A person who is successful breeds success.

The customer will be glad to see you if you are *up*. It helps lift his spirits. Customers like to deal with successful people—not losers.

A smile is an extension of good feelings you have inside of you. Make the sales call as fun and as enjoyable as appropriate.

Set the stage. Become an extension of your solution. It's up to you to stimulate, activate, and motivate. Hold on to an infectious belief in what you are selling, and act out your excitement.

In my younger days, I used to enjoy watching the Friday night fights on television with my father.

One of the sponsors of those fights was the Gillette Razor Blade Company. Gillette had a jingle that always stayed with me. It went something like this:

> YOU WANT TO LOOK SHARP . . .
> YOU WANT TO FEEL SHARP . . .
> YOU WANT TO BE SHARP . . .

In essence, that message is what Positive Contact is all about. Looking sharp is your appearance. Feeling sharp is your attitude. Being sharp is your energy.

All of these elements represent Positive Contact.

7

The Fifth Strategy for Positioning:
Get Organized!

I've seen it happen too often.

A bright, eager graduate at the top of his class joins a dynamic sales organization—and he's at the head of everyone's "watch 'im" list.

The word is out: He's gonna *go!* He's gonna be terrific.

For a while, he's the office darling. Everyone has high hopes and expectations for this person.

But it gradually becomes apparent that Tom or Stan or Molly isn't doing so well. The writing is on the wall. You can hear it in the buzz of conversation around the office:

"What's happening? Why isn't he taking off? What's wrong?"

There's a gradual deterioration of status until the fair-haired boy falls out of favor and his name no longer graces the lips of his many sponsors and well-wishers.

And in the end, this person eventually winds up leaving the organization.

It's impossible to generalize about situations like this, familiar though they may be. There are as many reasons for failing to achieve as there are individuals who have failed.

But frequently I've discovered that potential achievers—those who really *could* excel if they would cross certain hurdles—fail to live up to expectations for one fundamental reason: they *never get organized!*

One salesman I counseled remains vividly in my memory, though I worked with him more than a dozen years ago.

Perry Gillard was a salesman for the Mead Corporation. A family man with many outside interests, Perry was a skier, bridge player, and Little League coach. In fact, at the time I first met him, Little League was one of his consuming passions. Around the office, when he wasn't complaining about his lousy job or bragging about his accomplishments, he was talking Little League to anyone who would listen.

Perry's problem was this: His life was so full of outside interests that he had no time for work.

He was running around the sales track with no finish line in sight.

He was winging it on every sales call.

And he was paying a high price for not being organized.

Around the office, behind his back, people called him "The Roadrunner." Beep-beep—and he was off. Just let him sniff a new lead and he was after it. The word was that he wore out four sets of tires a year driving around to call on new accounts. He planned his visits like a blindfolded person swatting flies.

He would make dozens of calls a day. As one person put it, Perry was capable of more, but occasionally a customer would slow him down by asking him what he was selling.

His sales pattern looked like a bronco at a rodeo show. He was Don Quixote attacking windmills.

It was almost funny.

But not quite.

Perry Gillard was about to be fired.

At that time I was the Mead sales trainer, conducting seminars and traveling around the country calling on key accounts. One of the regional managers asked whether I would have a conversation with Perry—as a kind of last-resort gesture. He really didn't expect an overnight change, but someone had to tell Perry that it was time to get better or get out.

So I was the lucky one chosen to counsel Perry.

I caught him early in the morning—all ready to rush out the door.

"Hey, Perry, let's have a talk," I said. A short way into the conversation, I asked, "Do you know what's happening to you?"

And it was a good thing no one else was in the office. By the time we finished talking about it, Perry Gillard was in bad shape.

I put it to him as gently as I could.

But I didn't withhold the truth.

I finished by saying, "It's a good thing you have Little League—because you need it. It's giving you everything you're not getting on the job. There's a way to get better. But if you're going to get better, you have to *get organized.* And no one can do that for you."

Fortunately Perry's new sales manager at that time was a great people-developer, Tom Costello—the very best of Mead's hand-picked "youth corps" of MBAs.

Costello was willing to take the time and exercise the patience to help get Perry on track.

We were using a plan that today I call the *Strategic Selling Plan.* Tom sat Perry down with the Strategic Selling Plan—and had him develop one for each of his prospective accounts:

- Whom are you calling on?
- What are you trying to accomplish?
- What's your objective with this account?
- What specific needs do they have?
- What do you propose to do to respond to their needs?
- What's their reaction to you thus far?
- What are the problems and opportunities in this account?
- What's your next step?
- And what can I do to help?

In addition to making Perry consider his goals with the target account, Costello also made him take a hard look at the larger picture—the importance of that account in relation to others.

Costello made Perry *fill out,* by hand, every blank in the Strategic Selling Plan for each target account. Perry did not approach these accounts until he had a well-thought-out purpose for making the call. He had to say in advance what he hoped to accomplish and how he planned to achieve his sales-call goals.

Perhaps the best way to sum up what happened is to note the change I saw in Perry Gillard when I saw him some months later.

He had a undergone a *physical* change.

He wasn't bouncing off the walls anymore. His jumpy, fidgety manner had been replaced by a calmness and serenity that weren't there before.

He talked less. He stopped blaming people. He wasn't spending as much time in coffee shops whining. And he didn't brag as much. He had an inner air of confidence that needed less of an overt display.

You could actually see the change in Perry Gillard.

The change in his demeanor had a measurable impact on the

people around him—and on his sales results. He went from being the enthusiastic bandleader who jumps on every wagon, to being a polished, confident model of selling.

The end result was almost unbelievable.

The salesperson who had come within a hair of being fired became the *standard of excellence* in his organization.

In a way, I identified with Perry Gillard, because I'd known what it was like to have a ready-fire-aim approach to selling.

On my first job, when I was working for Harry "the Horse" Goldman, he called me into his office and asked me, "Young man, how long have you been here?"

"Thirteen months, Mr. Goldman."

"And what should that tell you, young man?"

"I don't know, Mr. Goldman. What *should* it tell me?"

"It should tell you that we've been carrying you longer than your *mother*. And furthermore, your next raise will become effective as soon as you do."

In those days it was a criticism I deserved, because I didn't really have any plan at all. My sales calls were all push-and-pull affairs because I had no clear-cut objectives.

Recently, I saw a production of *A Chorus Line,* and I was struck by the powerful and moving words of one of the members of the chorus line. He says:

"I had no plan, no alternative. I just wanted to get through the day."

There are many salespeople who would identify with those words. When we have no plan and no alternatives, all we want to do is to get through the day.

The Strategic Selling Plan is a key strategy that I co-developed with my associate, Joe Cascarelli, who has been instrumental in making the plan meaningful to thousands of salespeople.

For many salespeople, this selling plan has been a way out of the woods. When you have the plan in front of you, you don't have to worry about what you do every day. Your *objectives, strategies,* and *action steps* are clearly outlined in front of you.

Your *objective* is a concrete, measurable result to be achieved by a specific date. For example, an *objective* might be:

> To increase our industrial line business 20 percent with the Atlantic Corporation by December 1.

A *strategy* is a general course of action to be pursued to reach your particular *objective.* For example, in order to increase your business at Atlantic, your strategy is to:

> Create Atlantic's awareness of a gap between the production methods they're currently using and the results they can achieve by adopting our Exeter 4000 line assembly system.

An *action step* is the specific activity that begins to implement the *strategy.* For example:

> Set up a meeting with Henry
> Carter, the plant engineer, for
> the purpose of identifying the
> production quota for the next
> three months.

It may take two or more individual action steps to implement your strategy and achieve your objective.

For me and for many other salespeople, I find that it's important to *write down* the activities that I'm engaged in throughout the course of a customer call. For this purpose I have a Strategic Selling Plan folder for each client—with the selling plan in a clear visual format on the outside of the folder. (This one works for me. You can add any other elements to make it more suitable to your sales setting.)

Strategic Selling Plan

Account Name: _____   Description of Organization: _____
Address: _____   _____
                                 _____
Phone: _____   _____

Account History: _____   Current Activity: _____
_____   _____
_____   _____
_____   _____

COMPETITIVE INFLUENCE:

Name	Activities	Reputation
_____	_____	_____
_____	_____	_____

DECISION INFLUENCERS:

Name and Title	Critical Concerns
_____	_____
_____	_____
_____	_____
_____	_____

Assessment of Situation: _____
_____
_____

Problems: _____   Opportunities: _____
_____   _____
_____   _____

OBJECTIVE: Concrete Measurable Result to Be Achieved by a Specific Date
_____
_____

STRATEGY: A General Course of Action to Be Pursued to Achieve the Objective
_____
_____
_____

Filling out the Strategic Selling Plan helps you think through what you want to do with the buyer.

It gets you focused. When you have a little break and you're thinking about the account, you have a *mental image.* If you write it down, on paper, you have a *visual image.*

Because of the selling plan's layout, you can center on opportunities and problems, and you can quickly assess the situation you find yourself in.

The Strategic Selling Plan helps you *remember* the content of the discussions you've had in the account and *record* them in such a way that they will be useful to you in the future.

Whenever you have to communicate vital account information to people within your organization, such as the manager of the marketing department, the Strategic Selling Plan helps you relay that information in a complete and easily understood format.

Contained in each Strategic Selling Plan is a record of your action steps, with an objective alongside each one, and an area to make note of results and follow-through activities.

Using this format keeps you on track in each sales call by reminding you of your objectives. And it forces you to look at each call in terms of the *results* that you produce.

When you think of your accounts in terms of the Strategic

Action Steps				Results Tracking	
Date	#	Action Step	Objective	Results	Follow-through

Selling Plan, your objectives, strategies, and action steps will always be clear to you.

When you execute the Strategic Selling Plan, you are always doing one of two things. Either you're gathering information to find out what the customer needs. Or else you're delivering information to respond to those needs and give him what he wants.

The two primary selling strategies that help you achieve these goals are the Gap and the Diamond.

The Gap and the Diamond are a package deal—you can't have one without the other. The Gap is the *diagnostic* process that you use to identify the customer's needs. The Diamond is the *treatment* process that enables you to present a solution and respond to those needs.

In the next two Strategies for Positioning, *Find the Area of Opportunity* and *Make the Customer Part of the Solution,* we will look at the dynamics of the Gap and the Diamond and find out what they can do for you. These are the graphic models that illustrate the flow of procedure, process, and method. They help you concentrate and focus your energy—and they prevent you from falling asleep at the switch.

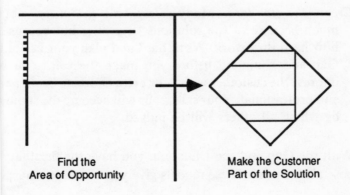

Find the
Area of Opportunity

Make the Customer
Part of the Solution

Because you have a plan and a process, you will have the ability to modify and adjust to the changing dynamics in the selling situation.

THIS IS NOT THEORY—IT'S ACTION-PLANNING.

Anybody can do what's natural. But to sit down and think about what you are going to do in a sales call, that's another thing! It takes forethought, discipline, and effort.

As you apply the Gap and the Diamond, keep the following ideas in mind:

Be yourself in the process. Who else is better qualified? These models are designed to help you structure the interaction between you and the customer. They are not designed to "put a lid" on your style and personality. Let the real you shine through and you will relate authentically.

Be flexible—choices give you power. Because you are dealing with the customer's individual inner dynamics, be flexible in using the Gap and the Diamond. Remember that built into these models are choices. Pay attention to how the customer is reacting and use the models to help you choose the best options. Options give you personal power and a broader range of responses.

Create the standard. Many salespeople get orders not so much because of the solutions they offer but because of how hard they work. Work hard and plan your use of the Gap and Diamond before you make the call. You will impress the customer with your extra efforts to be prepared and professional. Your sales calls will become the standard by which all others will be judged.

With the Gap and the Diamond, you have the flexibility to choose alternatives. These models give you a concrete purpose

for every sales call and a road map to help you get from Point
A to Point B. They are the tools that allow you to *get organized*,
to implement the Strategic Selling Plan, and to achieve your
sales call objectives.

8

The Sixth Strategy for Positioning:
Find the Area
of Opportunity

From 1973 to 1975, I was in charge of training a large number of U.S. Marine Corps recruiters in various parts of the country.

That was a terrible time to sell the Marine Corps to anyone. The Vietnam War was still on and antimilitary sentiment ran high on the college campuses. Recruiters, as the most visible representatives of the military, took the brunt of the abuse. Not only were they scorned and ridiculed by students on many campuses, they also had to face administrators, teachers, and counselors who insulted them, called them names, and ordered them off the premises.

In these years, recruiting for the U.S. Marine Corps was, without doubt, the toughest sell in the country. As one recruiter put it, "It was easier to sell diphtheria than to sell a hitch in the Marines."

In those late Vietnam years, the Marine Corps was *not* the answer to every young person's dreams. You couldn't sit down with a candidate and say, "Here are your choices, these will be your obligations, and you will be compensated in the following ways. Now, if you'll just sign here . . ."

We couldn't sell a ready-made solution.

We had to sell *opportunities.*

And to do that, we had to help young men recognize *what* were the areas of opportunity *for them.* So we *asked* them two simple questions:

1. What's important to you in the future?

   • The excitement of travel and adventure?
   • Expert training in a technical field?
   • Valuable leadership skills?
   • Advanced-education opportunities?
   • Steady income-advancement and security?

2. Where are you now in relation to your goals?

Once those questions were asked, it would be typical for a recruit to say, "That's why I'm here today—to find out how I can reach my goals."

In other words, each recruit began to recognize that there was a *gap* between what was happening now and what he needed. The more he talked about himself and his objectives, the clearer it became that he would have to do something to *close* that gap if he was going to succeed in reaching his goals.

In our conversations with these young men, the natural follow-up would be, "Now let me present the opportunities that exist in the Marine Corps to *close that gap* and help you achieve your objectives."

Presenting it that way, we were selling *something else* besides the Marine Corps.

WE WERE SELLING THEM ON THEIR OWN POTENTIAL.

We actually helped young men and women determine where they were going with their lives. Instead of reciting a litany of random information, we were helping individuals determine *desired outcomes* in their career paths.

The Gap is a model that I developed during my years as a sales trainer for the national and international divisions of the Mead Corporation.

This strategy was the result of hundreds of interviews that I conducted in the United States, Switzerland, Austria, Portugal, and other parts of the world where Mead sells products.

Everywhere I went, I asked salespeople to tell me what they *most* wanted to learn. Almost without exception, their priorities were the same:

- Teach us how to handle objections.
- Teach us how to close.
- But most of all, *please* teach us how to make an effective initial sales call.

Later on, when I was teaching Positional Selling strategies to business professionals at Xavier University in Cincinnati, I conducted a similar survey. The results were the same. For nearly all these business people, making effective initial sales calls was their most serious concern.

The Gap is a strategy that responds to this universally agreed-to priority:

IT IS THE KEY POSITIONING STRATEGY
FOR AN INITIAL SALES CONTACT.

I know a lot of salespeople who term these *cold calls*. And in many cases, that's exactly what those calls turn out to be—a chilling experience.

But when you use the Gap, you can turn a *cold call* into a *warm call,* because it's a strategy that gets you in touch with the buyer at the human level.

- It gives you time the buyer didn't want to give you.
- It introduces you to his Operating Reality.
- It gets you farther faster than any other sales activity you can use—while still enabling you to build a long-term relationship.

Too often, salespeople try to sell products, programs, or services on the basis of facts alone. They are preprogrammed (often by their own companies) to make high-powered presentations describing in great detail the benefits of what they have to offer—before discovering what their customers might possibly want or need. They treat their customers like an attentive audience tuned in to a commercial radio station.

But there's a serious flaw in this strategy.

Think about it: Would you try to sell someone a vacation in the Bahamas by telling him the price of the airline tickets, the dimensions of the hotel room, the length of travel time, and the daily tide tables? True, these are all relevant facts. But they have nothing to do with the real reason someone would want to go to the Bahamas.

What you're really selling is *one full week of rest and relaxation in a balmy island paradise.* In other words, a greater sense of well-being.

Now for the real challenge—getting the people you're selling to tell you what's important to them.

In the past, many salespeople subscribed to the belief that "selling is telling." So they would engage in information-dumping, overwhelming their customers with capability presentations. Or they would ask loaded questions, designed to lead the customer to a predetermined conclusion.

These short-term strategies of information-dumping may get your foot in the door, but they do not help you build and maintain a long-term relationship.

If you use an exploratory process *instead* of information dumping, you focus on what the customer *needs,* compare it to *what he's getting now,* and *reveal the Gap* that lies in between.

Whatever you're selling, you need the customer's help to understand what's important to him. You really have to find out two things from the customer:

"What do you need?"

and

"What's happening now?"

Then listen.

And if you listen and understand well enough, you will earn the right to present a solution that responds to the customer's needs.

How do you find the Gap?

It all depends on what you're selling.

A real estate agent asks his clients . . .

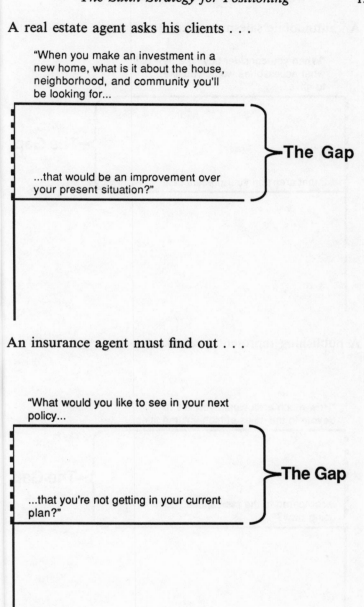

"When you make an investment in a
new home, what is it about the house,
neighborhood, and community you'll
be looking for...

...that would be an improvement over
your present situation?"

The Gap

An insurance agent must find out . . .

"What would you like to see in your next
policy...

...that you're not getting in your current
plan?"

The Gap

An automobile salesman needs to establish . . .

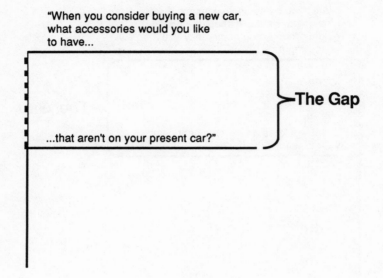

"When you consider buying a new car,
what accessories would you like
to have...

...that aren't on your present car?"

The Gap

A publishing representative asks . . .

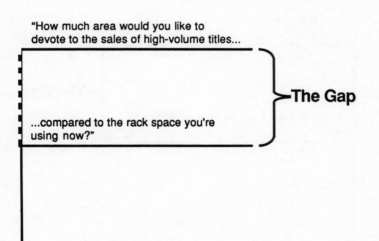

"How much area would you like to
devote to the sales of high-volume titles...

...compared to the rack space you're
using now?"

The Gap

A stockbroker needs to find out . . .

"What proportion of your total investments
would you like to go into high-risk,
high-return securities...

The Gap

...and how much of your money is
placed in these kinds of investments
at the present time?"

A salesperson for computer systems asks . . .

"When you establish your goals for
productivity, what kind of an
information-gathering system
do you anticipate needing...

The Gap

...and what are the characteristics
of your current system?"

The effective use of the Gap isolates and defines the buyer's needs. It takes you one step closer to the presentation of your solution—which I'll describe in the next chapter. But you can't leap into a presentation until you are certain that the customer *recognizes the Gap* and is willing to find a way to *close that Gap*.

By establishing a Gap, you draw his attention to the fact that he's not getting everything that's possible.

The fact is, when you're exploring the customer's needs—and not just information-dumping or probing—the customer will be interested in the solution. In some cases, the customer may even *anticipate* the solution. That's because he *learns from the process*. In any case, you are optimizing the customer's commitment to your solution by making him a part of the process of discovering his needs.

When I was counseling the Mead sales team, I accompanied a friend of mine, Bobby Bullock, in calling on a buyer named Aaron Wasserstrom. The company was Slant-Finn, one of America's leading manufacturers of baseboard radiators.

Wasserstrom was a tough, major-league, results-oriented buyer. You really had to *produce the goods* if you wanted him to keep you on as a supplier. It was a target account that Bullock put at the top of his "want-to-have" list.

As Bobby and I were waiting, Wasserstrom's secretary came out and said, "Gentlemen, he'll see you now, but I'm afraid it will have to be short. One of our other buyers is away on vacation and Mr. Wasserstrom is pinch-hitting for him. He can only give you ten minutes."

The office was cavernous. It seemed as though it took two of our ten minutes to cross the room and shake hands. Mr. Wasserstrom was a hard-hitting guy who made his presence felt the minute we entered his office. The first words out of his mouth were, "You guys better make it quick. I'm jammed up and I don't have much time for you."

I wondered how Bullock was going to handle this.

After a brief introduction, Bobby Bullock leaned forward confidently and stated, "Mr. Wasserstrom, if we're going to bring you some value for the time you're investing in us today, that value will not necessarily be achieved by our telling you all about our company. Instead I'd like to ask what's important to you when you consider a corrugated shipping container supplier?"

Mr. Wasserstrom looked Bullock in the eyes and said, "What's that again?"

"Mr. Wasserstrom," Bullock said, "what does a guy like me have to bring *you*—a buyer of boxes—in order to earn the right to your business?"

Mr. Wasserstrom contemplated that one for a moment.

Then he began talking.

Thirty-five minutes later, he was saying, ". . . and another thing I want from a supplier is a corrugated shipping container that has the strength of a two-by-four. I don't like to go out into my packing line and see boxes that look like graham crackers stuck in a glass of milk! Each time one of my packing lines goes down, I have forty-five workers standing around doing absolutely nothing at six dollars and thirty-five cents an hour! And when that happens, it's like spilling your coffee into the cash register, it runs into money! My packing line was down three times in the last month. I can't *begin* to tell you how much that cost me."

He caught his breath, leaned forward, and went on, "Another thing, I want salespeople calling on me who have the guts to call me up and tell me when they're going to be shipping me late. And I want salespeople who care enough to throw a few boxes in the back of the station wagon and deliver them out here to help me keep my line going—you know what I mean—to help me out of a jam."

Mr. Wasserstrom's voice rose: "I had a guy who used to be

a supplier here—but he's no longer a supplier because every time I had a problem he never answered the phone. He would always farm out his complaints to somebody else. He's no longer here because that guy caused me all kinds of problems. So I got rid of him!"

Mr. Wasserstrom went on like this for a little while longer, and when I glanced at my watch I saw that nearly *forty-five* minutes had now passed.

When Mr. Wasserstrom was finished, Bobby Bullock nodded.

"Mr. Wasserstrom," he said, "it's very clear by virtue of what you've just told me that there's a gap between what you *expect* from your suppliers and what you're currently getting. Because I have a substantial technical background and because I'm committed to earning the right to your business, *may I have the opportunity to see what I can do to close that gap?*"

And Aaron Wasserstrom said . . . *"Yes!"*

Bobby Bullock continued to follow up, and within three months he had cracked that account.

Essentially, one question was all it took.

But it had to be the right question.

If Bobby had started off the sales call with an extensive statement of his company's capabilities, by saying, "I want to tell you something about our organization and our program," he would have gotten nowhere.

Mr. Wasserstrom would have said, "Thank you very much for coming in, gentlemen. But the ten minutes are up."

Aaron Wasserstrom was an experienced buyer with a fine-tuned internal crap detector. My guess is he would have looked at Bobby Bullock with space-invader eyes, catalogued him with the thirty-five other box salespeople who called on him regularly, after which he would have given Bobby the shuffle-off-to-Buffalo.

But by posing a carefully considered information-gathering question, Bobby Bullock initiated a process that was *entirely in Aaron Wasserstrom's Operating Reality.* He found the Area of Opportunity.

I've seen this experience repeated many times. The Gap helps you *get* time the buyer *didn't mean to give you* on the initial sales call.

When you use the Gap, you are asking the buyer for a chance. Sometimes, of course, you'll get shot down. But you can write a lot of new business if you know the right questions to ask . . . *and then ask them!*

Be creative in your use of the Gap. *See* what you're saying. Keep an image of the Gap in your mind as you begin the exploratory process:

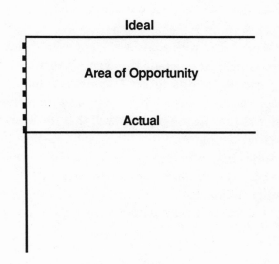

When you do that, you will know exactly what to do on the sales call. Keep in mind the three important things that you hope to accomplish in the exploratory process: what the buyer *needs*, what he *has*, and *what you can do to close the Gap*. At any given time during an exploratory sales call, you should be engaged in one of these three activities.

Jeannie Curtis, a young woman who works for Lance Jackson & Associates, one of the fastest-growing marketing agencies in Denver, has had great success with the Gap. Unlike many agencies that overwhelm potential clients with capability presentations as part of their initial effort to crack the account, Jeannie initiates her client contacts with a series of Gap-finding questions:

"Ideally, what kind of market are you trying to reach?"

"What image do you want to create in the eyes of the buying public?"

"What do you see as your current image?"

Her first interview with a client is spent asking questions like this. Even though she is selling the agency's services, she makes *no selling statements* during her Gap-finding activities.

But when the agency is ready to respond with a presentation, it understands the client's goals so well that the agency presentations are *on the mark*.

The result is that even though the initial interviewing process is quite extended, the time needed to present the solution is considerably reduced.

And the solution *always addresses* what's important to the client.

Not long ago, I was having lunch at Windows on the World with Bill Dwyer, the president and CEO of Moody's Investors Service.

As we were discussing sales training and practices, Bill asked me, "Jack, what do you think of intuition—the *inner knower* we all have that helps us understand things in general?"

"Bill," I replied, "I think intuition is absolutely essential. However, there's one thing I know for certain, and it's this—intuition always gets better with information."

When you use the Gap, you *gather* the information that helps your intuition get better.

When you ask responsible, serious questions, these questions should encourage the customer to dream out loud. From his replies, you come to know his hopes and expectations. As the customer answers, he realizes that there is a Gap between the results he is currently experiencing and those that he could be experiencing. By asking these questions, you help the customer open himself up to the ideas that will close the Gap between the old way of doing things and the better way that might be possible.

No matter how well you know the customer or how good your relationship is, you can't *assume* you know the Gap in the customer's Operating Reality. You need to ask the right questions to determine what he needs and where he is now in relation to those needs. By asking a question that focuses on certain needs—and listening carefully to his answers—you and the buyer may *both* find a Gap that you never anticipated.

Asking questions is not threatening. It's *how* you ask the questions that can be threatening. Your questions have to be *caring* and they have to be *supportive*. You can't probe the customer for information without telling him why you need that data and what you hope to do with it. You have to let the customer know, "I'm here to help you and I'm here to build a relationship on a solid foundation."

Recently I was visited in my office by a young man who wanted to sell me a new health insurance policy.

He was friendly and eager, but when he launched into a

series of personal questions, I felt as if I were getting the third degree.

He didn't tell me why he wanted certain information or what he was going to use it for. He didn't *stage* his questions. He just said he wanted to ask me some questions—and then he started in.

I felt as if I were in a line-up. He went through the seven levels of intimacy in about five minutes. The only question he didn't ask was whether my mother was expecting when she married my father.

Fifteen minutes into the conversation, he asked me how much money I made. I told him I thought this was proprietary information. I said I needed to know more about the importance and use of that information before I gave it to him.

Apparently my reply offended him. He made no attempt to reassure me. He told me that I had to be willing to give that information to him if he were going to suggest a plan or policy that would meet my needs. He said that because of my lack of openness with him, it appeared as if this sales call was going nowhere. He said he thought he was wasting his time and mine—and he got up and left.

After that call, I realized *I felt affronted* and pushed around. In reviewing what happened, it was clear that this person did very little to establish trust and put me at ease.

Had he indicated to me that he needed my help, that he might have been able to assist me, had he assured me that such information would be held in confidence and used to design a plan for my needs, then I would have responded much differently than I did.

If the salesperson's questions to a potential client are absent of any consideration—and if the questions are delivered in an insensitive, intimidating way—then count on the prospective buyer to clam up or "feed you a line" just to get rid of you.

•   •   •

When you're calling on a new prospect, it's essential to help the customer understand the purpose of your sales call *before* you begin to establish the Gap. Let the customer know how you plan to conduct the interview:

> "Carol, my purpose today is to find out whether the services my company has to offer would be useful to you. Before I begin to talk about my organization and what we can do, I'd like to develop a more complete understanding of your organization and your current needs. *I need your help to be successful.*"

Once you have established a climate of openness and cooperation, you are positioned to begin establishing the Gap.

Now, this isn't a *script*: it's a *tone.* And if you adopt a positive tone for positioning your particular organization, product, and services, I guarantee that the customer will respond favorably. Because the questions you're going to ask are in his or her interest, not your own!

The customer's reply always deserves an acknowledgment. After the customer provides you with information, show your appreciation:

> "Thank you for providing me with your views . . ."

> "According to what you're telling me, you see creative innovation as critical to increased productivity . . ."

> "Is my understanding correct?"

By posing your questions in this way, you avoid sounding like an interrogator. You let the customer know that his sharing is helpful to you in developing a keener understanding of his needs and in deciding how you're going to respond to them.

•　　•　　•

Occasionally, in using this strategy, you may encounter a buyer who says he's one-hundred-percent satisfied with his present situation. He does not perceive a Gap because he believes he is getting everything he needs from the results he's currently experiencing.

In that case, you can *add a dimension* by asking a question like the following:

"Terry, if after becoming acquainted with your present situation, we could add a dimension to the one-hundred-percent results you're currently experiencing, would you give me the opportunity to present an idea that I feel could make that happen?"

This is a *dimensional question.*

You can *visualize* this added dimension as an extension of the Gap:

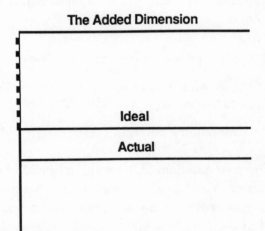

By suggesting an added dimension, you're actually issuing yourself a challenge. When the customer says, "Yes, I'd be open to seeing how we could get better results than we're currently achieving," it's up to you to *find a way* to make that happen.

It may not be easy to add a new dimension.

But in my experience, there usually *is* a way. It could be something distinctive and unique about your product, service, or organization—or, best of all, the extra, added value that *you* bring to the relationship.

Bringing a new dimension of value to the customer may be the best thing you ever did for him—or yourself.

Finding the Gap is the *diagnostic* process in Positional Selling. You don't have to *respond* to the customer's needs on the spot. In fact, if you present a solution prematurely—before you understand the Gap—you're jumping the gun.

In developing the Gap, I polled customer response throughout the United States and Europe to find out what people on the receiving end thought of it. The response from a variety of decision-makers was overwhelmingly favorable. Many customers told me that, for the first time, they felt the salesperson helped them discover what they were trying to accomplish.

Some comments on the exploratory process:

"It got to the point."

"It didn't waste my time."

"The salesperson paid attention to what's important to *me.*"

"I wasn't overpowered with a solution before he knew what my problem was."

The most challenging part of this process is to *listen*. Your questions give the customer the chance to come to his own conclusions about his current situation—and to see the possibilities that lie just beyond the horizon.

When you ask helping questions to find the Gap, you allow the customer to discover for himself that something's not right. Your questions give him the chance to come to his own conclusions about his current situation and his future possibilities. If you are listening rather than talking, the customer will see for himself the Area of Opportunity. And then, it's up to you to

MAKE THE CUSTOMER PART OF THE SOLUTION!

9

The Seventh Strategy for Positioning:
Make the Customer Part of the Solution

This strategy is dedicated to all those who, at some time in their lives, have tried to get someone else to *do something*.

During a normal, active day, there are many times when you're trying to get things done through other people. It could be you're trying to convince your spouse that it's time to buy a new car. Or you're trying to get your kids to be more attentive to their studies. Or you're trying to get your manager to support you in the solution of a problem.

The fact is, any time you're trying to convince someone to do something, you're *selling* that person. Somehow or other, you have to convince those people that what you want done is in their best interests.

As my youngest son, Kieran, once said, "Life is one big sales call."

When you're selling anything to people—an idea, a project, a task—you have to get them involved in the decision-making process so they will put their energy into making it work. You have to make them *part of the solution.*

In professional selling, a great deal of what you do in front of customers is *telling them* what you can do and how it will benefit them—and getting them to buy into the solution.

All your Gap-finding and support activities lead up to the delivery of the solution. This is where you get your customers to feel some ownership in the solution. They have to be convinced it's in their own best interests. You must energetically address your enthusiasm and frame your solution so that you're working on their behalf.

> *If you're soliciting a grant* and trying to get a committee to approve your proposal, you're selling. The committee's feeling of *ownership* in your plans and goals will have a lot to do with whether you're successful in getting that grant.

> *If you are the marketing rep* for a national hotel chain, you have to *match up* the features of your property with the needs of the meeting planner. You have to persuade the planner that your facility is better equipped to meet those needs than any competitive hotel chain.

> *As a salesperson of industrial machines,* you must convince the customer that your equipment has the production capacity that he insists on. Then, in a clear, easily understood manner, you have to present the customer with the *reason why* he ought to buy your machine rather than someone else's.

> *If you're selling a subscription* to a periodical, you have to convince the potential subscriber that the features and information contained in the magazine will respond to the reader's need to be entertained and kept informed.

If you are selling a health insurance plan to an organization, your presentation must take into account all the concerns the organization has for providing more complete coverage, a wider span of individual benefits, and greater ease in adjusting claims.

No matter what you're selling, one cardinal rule holds true: the more convinced *you are* that your product or service is the best, the more persuasive you will be.

But persuasiveness alone is not enough to sell the customer on the solution. You also have to be organized. The presentation must be made in such a way that the buyer understands *clearly* that you are in his Operating Reality the whole time—if you want to ensure a *commitment* from him.

THE PRESENTATION IS THE MOMENT OF TRUTH

Unfortunately, too many salespeople make sales presentations that are haphazard, random, and disorganized. Those presentations are like bowls of spaghetti. The salesperson throws in the spaghetti sauce, meatballs, sausage, porkchops, stirs it all around, opens up the customer's head, and drops it in. Then he expects the customer to run a rake through the mush, sort it out, and make sense of it.

Is it any wonder buyers are confused and become impatient?

It *should* be up to the *salesperson* to be organized. It's up to *you* to run the rake through the spaghetti before you serve it. And that means you have to straighten it out *in your own head* before you throw it on the plate.

In Positional Selling, we use the model of the Diamond to

straighten out a sales presentation and deliver it in such a way that it makes *sense* to the buyer.

The Diamond is based upon a widely used teaching strategy.

When you're addressing a class and you want to make sure the students are getting the same message and they all *understand* that message, what you do is:

1. Tell 'em what you're gonna tell 'em!
2. Tell 'em!
3. Tell 'em what you told 'em!

The Diamond is a complete visual summary of that teaching strategy. If you keep the Diamond in mind, you can *see* the presentation while you're *doing it.* The Diamond tells you *where you are* and *what comes next.*

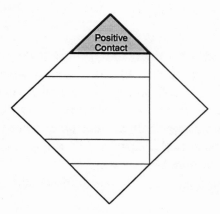

At the top of the Diamond is Positive Contact. That's Attitude, Energy, and Appearance. It's *bringing your energy to the customer.*

PROPOSAL STEP

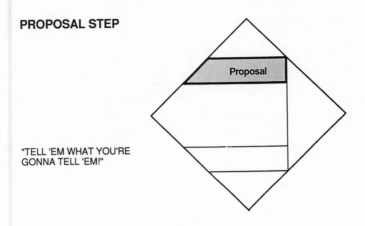

"TELL 'EM WHAT YOU'RE
GONNA TELL 'EM!"

Once you've established Positive Contact with some appropriate and interesting conversation, the next stage is the *task* part of the presentation. It's the Proposal step. This is where you *Tell 'em what you're gonna tell 'em*. In this step, you review the customer's needs that you uncovered during the exploratory process. Then you state your objective and make a direct Benefit Statement:

> "Carl, last time I was here, you expressed some concern about your current situation. You indicated that there was a gap between the results you're currently realizing and what you would like to see happen in the future. I am excited today, because my objective is to present you with a unique new idea that will close the gap and result in increased productivity and in market leadership."

Then move on to the Solution step. The Solution step consists of series of selling statements. It is in the selling statement that you present Features, Advantages, and Benefits. In other words, you *"Tell 'em!"*

SOLUTION STEP

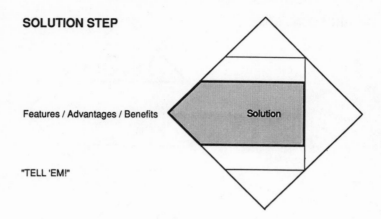

Features / Advantages / Benefits

"TELL 'EM!"

- Features—*What it is*
- Advantages—*How it works*
- Benefits—*What it's going to do to solve the problem and do the job*

Remember that, of all the points you make in the Solution step, the most important is the benefit. And a benefit, to be a benefit, has to answer the buyer's question:

"What does it do for me? Does your solution save me money, increase productivity, maximize profits, and make my life easier?"

It is in the benefits that you present the value of your solution as a more important asset than a lower price.

Back up your benefit statements with the appropriate use of evidence that your solution will work. Consider a testimonial, sales literature, a demonstration, samples, graphs, statistics, and visuals. This will add impact to your benefits by visually reinforcing your solution.

**SUMMARY AND
CLOSURE STEPS**

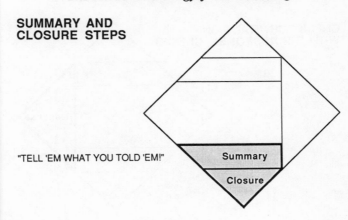

"TELL 'EM WHAT YOU TOLD 'EM!"

Then you move on to the Summary step. This is where you *Tell 'em what you told 'em!* And the best way to do that is to review the problem, restate the solution, and summarize the benefits:

"Tom, there is a gap. As I pointed out, our solution will close the gap, and you will experience the following benefits."

By summarizing the benefits, you make sure they are the last thing on the person's mind before you close.

When you move on to Closure, this is where you *Get 'em to do something about it!* Closure is getting the customer to buy into the solution and close the gap between what he *needs* and *what he's currently getting.*

The Diamond also includes a step that you can repeat many times throughout the presentation, and that's the *Response Check.* For salespeople, this is a critical element of the presentation process, because the Response Check tells you *how you're doing* during the presentation and lets you know *whether the customer is coming along with you.*

CHECK FOR VITAL SIGNS
WITH THE **RESPONSE CHECK!**

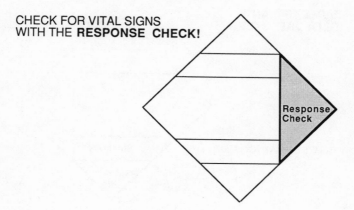

- Is the customer still there?
- Is he listening to you?
- Does he have hidden concerns?

The Response Check is like Mayor Koch saying, "How'm I doing?" with this difference: *You* have to be much more specific. Ask the buyer, "How does this solution meet the needs we discussed?" "Is there anything about the program, as I've presented it so far, that you'd like to ask about?" "Is there anything you'd like to *add?*" "How do you feel about the plan so far?"

The Response Check gives the customer a chance to become involved. You don't end up moving into a *Closure* when he's stalled somewhere back at the beginning with a nagging concern about something you mentioned during the Solution step. It opens *you* up for further information—if there is any. And it lets you uncover any hidden objections and address them directly (using LAER!).

When you use all the steps of the Diamond in your presentation, you . . .

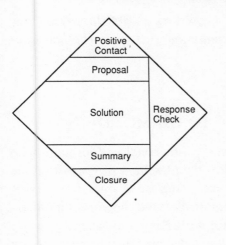

. . . create a climate of acceptance

. . . refocus on the need and create excitement and anticipation

. . . clearly outline your benefits and create a buy-in

. . . solicit customer reaction to the value of your solution

. . . review benefits before closing

. . . ask for a commitment

Now, you may ask, *What is the purpose of using a model?*

Well, if your spaghetti is well-organized, you don't *need* a Diamond—or any other model.

But I've found, over the years, that many salespeople make presentations *without any clear-cut plan of where they're going or how they're going to get there.*

For those salespeople who, like me, need a graphic road map to get where they're going, the Diamond is a *model* that keeps you on track and helps you to make highly focused, more professional sales calls.

And most important, when you use the Diamond to close the Gap, your presentation

MAKES THE CUSTOMER PART OF THE SOLUTION BECAUSE HE HELPED INVENT IT!

Salespeople who use the Diamond find that they achieve a whole new level of professionalism because they know what they want to achieve; they know how to get there; and they know how to make a presentation that squarely addresses what's important to the buyer.

FROM GAP TO DIAMOND

An outstanding young sales professional in Cleveland who had just been through the Positional Selling program told me about one of his first experiences using the Diamond—in a visit to the King Meat Packing Company—and the impact it had on this customer. His experience with King was, in many ways, typical of what happened again and again when he began to use the Gap and the Diamond in his sales presentations.

Blake Rhein was a sales representative for a data processing company that provides a wide range of computer services in payroll, accounting, and inventory. It was Blake's job to come in and sell the president and owners of the company on the computer services that Blake's company had to offer.

Blake's visit to the King Company had an inauspicious beginning. Entering through the side door of an abandoned-looking East Cleveland warehouse, Blake was ushered into a lobby that had the dimensions of a queen-size bed. To get to the owner's office, he had to walk through the freezer locker.

As he did so, he observed that the freezers were almost empty, and he wondered to himself how well the company was doing. So when he met Charlie Lauder, the manager of the company, Blake began the exploratory process by asking a general question about the current situation in the meat packing industry.

"Well," said Charlie in answer to Blake's question, "I don't know if you realize it, Blake, but right now our business could use a shot in the arm. People are not buying as much red meat as they used to. With the health craze in this country, people are staying away from red meat. And that's hurting our industry, of course."

Continuing the exploratory process with another question, Blake asked Charlie Lauder about his experiences with automatic data processing and his payroll system.

Charlie replied, "Blake, it's really very simple. I have four things that I need out of a system such as this. I need it to be *cost effective*. I need to *get my checks back on time*. I need it to be *accurate*. And I need it to *free up some time* for my own administrative person, Barbara Schwartz. She's swamped with accounts receivable and accounts payable, invoicing our customers—and trying to get them to pay their bills!

"Any new system has to be *cheap* for us to do," continued Charlie. "We can't pour a lot of funds into starting up a whole new system."

After exploring a few more areas of concern, Blake felt as if he had established the Gap—and he went directly into the Diamond, focusing on what the customer needed.

THE DIAMOND IN ACTION

In the Proposal step of the Diamond, Blake said, "O. K., Charlie, let me see if I understand you. You need the system to be reliable and accurate, you need the checks delivered on time, and you need it to be cost-effective. Is that right?"

"Yes, that's right."

"Well, I'm delighted to be here today, because I have a unique plan for you that can respond to those needs and provide you with significant cost and time savings."

Blake moved into the Solution.

"One of the features of our data processing is the turnaround time involved in getting you your checks. We have a *twenty-four-hour turnaround time*. And the advantage to you is that when you input to us, we'll have those checks back on your desk the next day, delivered by a bonded, full-time employee of our company. The benefit in this system is that it's going to save you and your employees *time* and *money*.

"Now the second feature of dealing with our data processing is ease of input. You simply call one of our operators, give that person the information about your payroll, it's verified on our computers, and then the operator will ask you to confirm all the information you've delivered.

"The advantage to this is that the information you give the operator is going to be very accurate because it's checked *at least two times.* With that kind of accuracy, we won't have to do reruns, which can waste a lot of your company time.

"Now the benefit to this is the cost-effectiveness of the system. I notice that you said your administrator, Barbara Schwartz, is very active and involved in accounts payable, accounts receivable, invoicing, and so forth. With our program, the result to you will be better use of Barbara's time and lower check-writing costs."

Finally Blake showed Charlie the forms and input documents that Barbara would use—and described how Blake's company would provide the *most cost-effective means* for Charlie to do his payroll.

Blake used a Response Check. "How does this sound to you, Charlie?"

Charlie had several concerns focused around the cost. Using LAER, Blake demonstrated that the value of the program would offset the cost—which satisfied Charlie's concerns.

In the Summary, Blake summarized the benefits by saying, "This will save you time and money."

He moved to Closure by asking, "When can I begin the implementation of this system within your organization?"

At this point, Charlie hesitated. He said he wanted to think about it and talk to his father who owned the company—they had some other quotes out and other considerations they wanted to take into account.

Blake replied, using LAER, "I understand your desire to talk this over with your father. Nonetheless, it appears to me from what you've said that you'll have a lot to say about the decision. Based upon what I've shown you, do you feel enthusiastic enough about the benefits of the program to recommend it to your father?"

Charlie was very positive and indicated that he would recommend the proposal to his father.

Blake set a time when he would call again.

When he got back to the office, Blake drew up a written version of the presentation in a letter that was hand-delivered to King Meat Company the next day.

Three days later, Blake followed up with a call to Charlie.

"Yes, Blake," Charlie told him, "I'm willing to go with this system."

And Blake set a time to meet again with Charlie Lauder to make sure the system was set up properly.

It was at this later meeting that Blake realized just how effective he had been on his previous sales call.

"You know, Blake," Charlie said to him, "you guys were a little bit more expensive than your competitors. But what made us go with this system was really *your presentation* and *the way you handled yourself with us.* We thought you were organized and demonstrated a real interest in our company.

"Do you know what the other guys did?" he went on. "They just came in here and spouted off about how great their companies were.

"They told us how wonderfully they were going to do our system—but they never really took the time to get to know us. They never really found out *what we do* or *how we do it!* And they never presented their program in a way that made any sense."

THE DIAMOND IS A QUALITY PRESENTATION

The fact that a company that was highly cost-sensitive would take a higher-priced program because of the quality of the presentation was a revelation to this young sales professional. Before he was introduced to Positional Selling, Blake was the type of salesperson who would walk in with a lot of literature and a pitch ten miles long. He would proceed immediately to tell his prospects what a terrific job he could do for them.

As Blake describes it, "I would go in and blast away on my prospects about how great *we* were without ever taking time to find out about *them*. In the past my presentations never really took their needs into account—much less involved the buyer in the process of discovering the solution.

"But I learned that blasting away got limited results!"

Blake was the kind of person who was naturally interested in other people and concerned about helping them. But all those concerns paled beside the need for a commission check. In order to do the best he could for himself *and* his customers, he needed a structure that would give him confidence that he was doing the right thing.

The Diamond provided that structure.

The Gap and the Diamond always go hand in hand. The Gap is a *diagnostic* process, whereby you establish critical concerns and find out what the buyer *needs*. The Diamond is the *treatment* process, where you respond to those needs and *make the customer part of the solution*.

As Blake's experience shows, the Gap has to be established before you use the Diamond. If you do the Diamond without the Gap, you're a *solution in search of a problem*. You'll end up digging a hole for yourself if you try to present a solution without *first* finding the Area of Opportunity.

Whenever you're making a presentation, you have to be constantly alert to *buying signals* from the customer. Be ready to respond to those buying signals appropriately.

The model of the Diamond is meant to help you stay on track. It's not meant to be a rigid system, putting you into a lock-step monologue. The Diamond is flexible. Be alert to what the buyer is saying. If your five senses tell you the customer is ready to close, be ready to take the order at any time.

In other words, when you're making a presentation,

KEEP THE COTTON OUT OF YOUR EARS!

Some years ago, I made a sales call on the Smith Scharff Paper Company in St. Louis, where I was meeting with Arthur Scharff, the president of the company.

I had made several telephone calls previously, to establish the needs of his organization (using the Gap) and to determine what he was looking for in a sales training program. So this call was primarily for a presentation—and of course I planned to use the Diamond.

Our meeting was held at an airport hotel. I took an early morning flight, and as soon as I arrived, Scharff said, "Carew, tell me about your program."

So after a brief recap of his company's needs, I told him what the program was, what it would do for him, and how he would benefit. I felt I was getting a reasonably positive buy-in.

But about a half-hour into the presentation, Scharff said he had to make some sales calls. So I had to cut it short—and I was only halfway through the Solution step.

Before he left for his next appointment, Scharff said to me, "Look, Jack, when are you flying out of here?"

"About two o'clock," I told him.

"Would you like to make some sales calls with me?" he asked.

I said, "Of course."

We got in his car, and while we were going to the first account, he said, "Tell me some more about Positional Selling."

So I made a few more selling statements while we were driving.

After we'd made a few calls, he said, "How about lunch? Do you like kosher?"

"I love kosher. What else? I'm from New York."

We went to a kosher deli on the outskirts of St. Louis, where we both ordered double hot-pastrami sandwiches with cole slaw and Russian dressing on a kaiser roll—and Diet Cokes (because we were both watching our weight).

And as I was chomping away on my double hot-pastrami and attempting to wipe the Russian dressing off my chin and slurping down Diet Coke between mouthfuls, I heard Arthur saying to me,

> "Jack, *when we do this program,* I want my father to be there because I would like him to be the person who introduces Carew Positional Selling to my sales team. So be sure, *when you schedule the program,* that you give me enough advance notice so that my father can be involved."

Now, within the framework of the Diamond, I had only completed the Solution step; theoretically I had two more steps to go: I had not yet done the Summary step—which was to remind him that he had certain needs, that the program would fill those needs, and then to summarize the benefits. And I should have gone into some kind of Closure with him.

But the sixty-four thousand dollar question is: Was it necessary?

When I heard the buying signal, I knew the other steps were

unnecessary because it was very clear that Arthur Scharff had already purchased the program!

The point is: Permit yourself to be updated by the buyer. If you pay attention to what the buyer says, you'll know what to do next. And the Diamond is always available to you to help you get back on track if you need it. But you've got to keep the cotton out of your ears.

Another thing I've learned about the Diamond: Don't allow yourself to be distracted from the purpose of your call.

STAY FOCUSED!

Frequently, I've been with a customer who had to leave the room for one reason or another, and he'd say:

> "Jack, it's perfectly all right to use my telephone and make a call if you have to. I'll be back in ten minutes. If you want to call your office, or whatever, go right ahead."

Once upon a time, I would always have taken advantage of opportunities like that. I'd run to the phone, call my office, say, "What's happening? How are things going? Any problems? Who called? What does he want?" And so forth.

Now, I resist the temptation.

If you call the office and get distracted by bad news, good news, messages, or whatever else is waiting for you back there, you may become *disoriented* or *distracted.* One piece of bad news, for instance, can blow your concentration out of the water. If that happens, you'll be in an entirely different mental state when the customer comes back.

It will be very difficult to pick up where you left off with the same enthusiasm.

For this reason I *always* counsel salespeople to think about *what* you were doing and *how* you were doing when the customer left. Then prepare yourself for his return.

Upon the customer's return, always remember to review what you've covered thus far and where you plan to go from this point on:

> "Julie, just before you left the room, we were discussing . . .
>
> "And now, what I plan to cover with you are the following topics. . . ."

The Diamond gives you a flexible structure for your sales call, and the great advantage of that structure is that you can pick up where you left off.

So be ready to *reposition yourself* in the framework of the Diamond when the buyer comes back into the room.

Close in depth.

You also have to think about the other people in the buyer's organization who are not in the room. The person you're talking to may have to sell to them in your absence. That means he needs to be prepared to make a presentation that will represent you even when you aren't there.

In other words, you have to *close in depth.*

Many times, when you're dealing with a large organization with many levels of decision-makers, you have to go into an Extended Close. You have to get the deal on the spot, but you also have to go after the person you have no access to. You cannot walk away from that responsibility. You have to get the person who's made the commitment to sell the *other* people energetically.

That's what I call *closing in depth.*

Before you let the buyer out the door, you should ask him, "What benefits of this program do you plan to sell to your associates? What questions are they going to raise that you have to prepare for ahead of time?"

You clear up all of that so that he becomes an extension of your presentation. He becomes *you in your absence.*

Sometimes in the middle of a presentation, you may feel as if you don't have the customer's attention. If you think you're losing the buyer, use the Response Check!

The Response Check can be an *open-ended question:* "What are your thoughts regarding this idea?" This gives you more than a yes or no answer.

Or a *closed question:* "Does this approach offer the solutions you're looking for?" To which the customer will typically respond with a "Yes" or "No."

Or just a *prolonged pause:* After you've made a key Benefit Statement, just pause for a second to see whether the buyer has anything to add. Give the buyer a chance to voluntarily come into the transaction.

Any kind of Response Check involves a certain risk. You're risking an objection. But if the customer *does* raise an objection, just handle it with LAER—Listen, Acknowledge, Explore, Respond.

A RESPONSE CHECK REDUCES YOUR INFORMATIONAL BLACKOUT.

With the Response Check you find out how the customer is digesting what you're telling him.

Many times, in a sales call, you really don't know where you stand, especially if you're calling on a Great Stone Face. This is the kind of guy who, when you say hello to him, is stuck for an answer. With that kind of person, we can never tell from his expression whether he's happy, sad, glad, or mad. So we lose a lot of energy trying to figure out where we stand with this person because we're not getting any feedback from the customer. We may assume that we're in trouble when in fact the call is going very well.

If you think the call is going downhill, and you don't validate that assumption with a Response Check, *the sales call could dribble off the edge of the table!*

Don't let that happen! Use the Response Check to audit the progress of the sales call and to make sure you know where you stand. If you're operating with misconceptions or false assumptions, you may find out, too late, that if you had asked for the order, you probably would have gotten it!

GO FOR THE CLOSE

There must be at least a hundred ways to put closure on the transaction.

The ones that I've found to be most universally effective are these:

A Direct Close is a high-risk close that gets to the point fast: "May I get started with an order today?"

An Indirect Close begins with an explanation: "Time is obviously a factor for you, so we should schedule delivery as soon as possible." And if you get no reaction, you follow up with a Direct Close: "May I proceed on that basis?"

The Choice Close assumes the customer has already bought in to the solution. Now you need some acknowledgment of that, so you ask, "Should we schedule implementation of the system immediately, or shall we wait until the early part of the week?"

The Benefit Close emphasizes, once again, the desired outcomes of your program. "Can we begin to reduce downtime and increase your profits today?"

The Next-Step Close—when you can't get a firm commitment on an order—asks for a commitment to some further action. "Inasmuch as we can't reach a decision today, may I recommend the following next step?"

Apart from these closes, challenge yourself to find ways to get the customer to make a commitment.

When you ask for an order, remain silent and patient. The ball is in the customer's court.

WHATEVER YOU DO, ALWAYS ALWAYS ALWAYS
ASK FOR THE ORDER!

If you come to the end of your presentation and wonder whether to go for closure—*don't wonder!—GO FOR IT!*

H. Ross Perot, the phenomenally successful supersalesman who created Electronic Data Systems (EDS) of Dallas, once tried unsuccessfully to send two planeloads of Christmas gifts and food to P.O.W.s in North Vietnam. During an interview about that failed attempt, the newscaster made a point of saying that Perot had attempted an *impossible* feat.

Perot replied, "It may have been impossible. But I believe it is better to have tried and lost than to live a life of silent desperation."

It's true in selling. I think it's better to have asked for the order and have lost it than to go around wondering whether you *would* have been successful *if you had only asked!*

After you . . .

. . . Tell 'em what you're gonna tell 'em!

. . . Tell 'em!

. . . And tell 'em what you've told 'em!

. . . THEN ASK 'EM TO DO SOMETHING ABOUT IT!

Unlike horseshoes and hand grenades, coming close isn't enough. You have to be right on the mark.

And the Diamond puts you there!

10

The Eighth Strategy for Positioning:
Assume the Responsibility

Some friends and I go back a long way. When I see them, we talk easily about people, places, and events that we all know. We have many common reference points in our background. We have a *willingness* to share information. And that willingness to share information and trust becomes a lasting bond between us.

The same is true of the best buyer–seller relationships. Both you and the customer have information that could be vital to the other person. The buyer has his personal needs, values, and motivations—and you, the salesperson, have unique information that will help that person achieve his goals and will significantly improve the quality of his life.

But unless that body of information is *shared* and becomes common knowledge, you won't get off dead center. You will not be able to initiate a relationship.

Your objective is to expand your common ground.

If you can expand your understanding of what you're trying

to accomplish, then you have the beginnings of a relationship that's going to go someplace.

Shared knowledge is essential.

Mutual understanding is *critical* to the relationship.

It's your responsibility—not the buyer's—to *initiate* the process of sharing knowledge and increasing the area of mutual understanding. It's up to you to expand the area of the common ground.

To do that, you have two tools to help you—the Gap and the Diamond. The Gap is information-gathering—it helps you to expand the common ground by finding out more about the customer. The Diamond helps the customer find out more about *you*.

If you *balance* the use of the Gap and the Diamond, you and the customer both share information in a trusting manner.

But when you overuse one process model to the extent of underusing the other, a *lopsided* relationship emerges.

Salespeople then fall into three commonly known, but not-appreciated stereotypes: the Presenter, the Interrogator, and the Visitor. Their inability to balance out the Gap and the Diamond prevents them from realizing their full potential in building lasting relationships.

Then there is a fourth type of salesperson who reaches maximum productivity and effectiveness by *balancing* the use of the Gap and the Diamond. This is the Producer.

THE PRESENTER

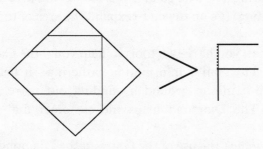

Too much Diamond. . . Too little Gap

A Presenter is a salesperson who *seizes control.*

He allows very little participation on the part of the buyer.

The excessive use of information-dumping has a steamroller effect on the buyer, who is *flattened out* by an avalanche of product and service information.

As a result, the buyer feels left out and not responsible for anything. His importance is reduced. He doesn't feel as if his needs are being taken seriously, and he has very little ownership in the solution.

Recently, I accompanied a very aggressive salesperson for a medical products firm on a sales call. He was seeing several administrative personnel of a large hospital system.

Jay Weston had built up a head of steam, and he couldn't stop. He was filled with product information—and he literally *overwhelmed* the hospital administrators with an onslaught of technical information. It was a tidal wave sales call.

Jay had all the supports he needed to back him up—photographs, diagrams, quality control reports, mechanical design specs, and testimonials—and by the time he was finished, he had shown the administrators everything.

Not only that, Jay asked for the order *five times*.

And when the decision-makers said they would like to talk it over, Jay offered to leave the room for *a few minutes* while they reached their decision.

By then, I could clearly see the impact that Jay's behavior was having on his prospective client.

The people in that room felt *overwhelmed, pinned down,* and *pressured.*

They were being strong-armed by Jay, and they knew it. They felt muscled into making a buying decision.

And with only a few minutes to consider making an order, they quite understandably refused to make a commitment.

Jay is the perfect example of an extreme Presenter, caught up in the arrogance of his solution.

This is a salesperson who engulfs the customer with product information.

The Presenter makes sales calls with a sledge hammer in his attaché case. He beats his potential clients into submission with a barrage of endless reasons why they should adopt his product or service without ever really understanding their needs.

The Presenter sees his sales call as an inspirational road show with him as the star attraction.

He's a solution in search of a problem and doesn't want to be confused with how the buyer feels about the solution because he's already got his mind made up.

THE INTERROGATOR

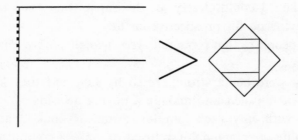

Too much Gap...Too little Diamond

An Interrogator, on the other hand, often comes on with a low-key, searching sales call. He'll frequently nod his head and say things like, "Oh, isn't that interesting?"

Being in the presence of this kind of salesperson is like going to confession.

Then, the Interrogator becomes a *prober*—attacking with questions but providing very little reassurance that the information he receives will help him respond to your needs.

In fact, his questions are so detailed that frequently the Interrogator makes the buyer feel ignorant, ill-informed, or unprepared for not having the answers.

Often the Interrogator uses his detailed questions as a subtle way of advertising his product expertise.

Some sales environments lend themselves to questioning activities. In insurance, financial counseling, or any kind of consulting work where a lot of sensitive information is required, it's imperative to guard against becoming an Interrogator. It is in these sales arenas that you have to avoid using the hammer-and-chisel method for obtaining information.

When I think of an Interrogator, I am reminded of the time the Fiat Metal Company retained the services of one of the Big Eight accounting firms to do productivity studies. The firm was represented by a man named Walter Johnson who was to interview people at Fiat to gather information and then make recommendations.

Most organizations know they're going to have to share proprietary information when a consultant is called in. But Walter made you feel as if you were getting the third degree because he attacked you with questions that could put your colleagues on the spot.

As soon as you were seated, he would ask:

"What don't you like about working around here?"

"Is your boss giving you the kind of support you need to get the job done?"

"What could your boss do to make you feel more appreciated?"

"If you could be more productive, what would you do to improve your work habits?"

He would engage people in an endless line of questions. He made people feel defensive and put them on the spot because they thought they would be hurting their friends. He was supposed to be gathering information to help the company perform better. But his proposed solution was faulty because they were giving him wrong information.

His questions were not *helping questions,* they were *scolding questions*—and people reacted accordingly. They gave him information that was in *their* best interests and not necessarily the company's. By acting like an Interrogator, Walter significantly diminished the value of his firm's recommendations because he did not earn the support of Fiat's employees in trying to make the solution a success.

If you just ask a lot of questions and don't tell the customer why you need that information, the person begins to wonder, "What does he want all that data for?" Quite justifiably, he begins to think to himself, "Well, I'm telling you a lot, but what are you *doing* with what I'm *telling* you?"

If you're an Interrogator, you don't come across as *interested*—you come across as *nosy.* And as a result, the customer becomes cautious and suspicious. He starts giving you misleading or inaccurate information just because he resents the intrusion.

THE VISITOR

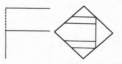

Very little Gap...Very little Diamond

A Visitor is the salesperson who doesn't *actively* dig in and acquire customer information—nor does he have a method for presenting new products, introducing new ideas, and gaining a commitment.

He seems quite satisfied with maintaining the status quo.

He's like a shadow—he leaves no footprints in the snow.

This kind of person makes content-free sales calls.

He resists conflict and serious business-related discussions at all costs.

I was once acquainted with a salesman by the name of Mark Arnold, who sold advertising premiums and promotional specialties such as plaques and incentive awards.

Typically, he would bring in a lot of samples and leave them with me. Then he would ask me to show the samples around to the other people in my company.

He would tell me, "I'll call you next week, and you can tell me what your people like."

And just as certainly, I would have my secretary pack up his samples and ship them back to him.

Often, he would give away half of his samples to people he was selling to. He wouldn't even bother to pick up what he'd left behind.

Mark Arnold was a typical Visitor. He was constantly running away from the possibility of rejection. He had a very strong need for acceptance and didn't want to risk offending anybody. He counted on *time* to be his ally, telling himself, "If I see enough people and *I'm a nice guy,* sooner or later someone will give me a shot at the business."

The Visitor is a time sponge. He and the hours in the day are expendable. He throws his watch away on every sales call and costs the customer valuable time without giving anything in return. He makes a lot of cotton-candy sales calls—mostly air. He doesn't find out enough about the customer's needs to be helpful, nor does he present viable reasons why anyone should buy what he's selling.

When he's gone, the customer sees that nothing has been accomplished—and nothing happens. A pleasant interlude has taken place—and that's about all.

THE PRODUCER

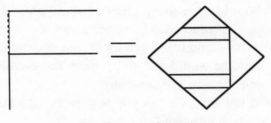

Equal Gap. . . and Diamond

The Producer *balances* the use of the Gap and the Diamond. He is concerned with *productivity* rather than *activity*. A Producer who is observant and concerned remains open to customer needs.

He sees information as essential to developing an accurate accounting of buyers' needs. And his presentation *credits* the client for his part in providing an understanding of what's important to that client. The Producer is a *team player*, and he recognizes that he can only be as successful as the buyer will let him be.

A very good friend of mine and the president of Insinger Machine Company, Rob Cantor, is a great salesperson because he is a great Producer. Rob exercises the kind of flexibility that it takes to work effectively with people and be alert to their needs—and he provides solutions that are in his customers' Operating Reality.

Insinger Machine Company is a food service equipment manufacturer that sells its products through manufacturers' reps who handle a varied line of different products. Rob has to sell *his line* to the representatives who promote and sell his equipment.

At a recent dealer meeting in Chicago, Illinois, on a Monday night immediately following a long, boring speech by another equipment manufacturer, Rob found himself in front of a room full of dealers who were on the verge of falling asleep.

Rob immediately recognized that he would have to act fast if he wanted to wake them up and get their attention, so he asked:

"How many of you want to get out of here in time to see the ballgame?"

Followed by:

"How many of you want to make money?"

And his concluding question was:

"How many of you will go along with me if I show you how to make money and *still* get you out of here in time to see the ballgame?"

And of course, everyone agreed to that.

So Cantor *had their support* when he asked the next five questions:

"What do you see as your opportunities in the marketplace?"

"What are the barriers that are preventing you from seeing the success you would like to achieve?"

"How is the competition preventing you from being successful?"

"What can you, as dealer reps, do to get your fair share of the market?"

"What should *I* be doing to help you be successful?"

Rob got a variety of answers to the first four questions. But the reps were unanimous in their answer to the fifth: *"Bring us new products!"*

And in response to that request, Rob Cantor introduced a brand-new line of products for the coming year.

Before the salespeople left, Rob *pinned down* their commitment by saying, "Ladies and gentlemen, before we leave here tonight to watch the Monday Night game, I would like to know what accounts you will be approaching with our new line of food service equipment. And I want you to tell me what *I* can do to successfully support you in taking that product to the customer."

As a direct result of that meeting, Insinger Machine Company received hundreds of orders for its new equipment. And true to his word, Rob Cantor maintained a *consistent presence* in his dealer relationships and provided support in every possible way for the sales efforts of those dealers.

Rob Cantor handles *all* his sales calls like a Producer. He gets into the Operating Reality of his customers by identifying what they really want. He gets *them* to identify their needs by asking questions that establish the Gap. And then he *closes* the

Gap by presenting exactly what his customers want. He gets a commitment from his customers to take the next step, while he promises his complete support for their future sales efforts. They respond to him because he always follows through.

Every salesperson has it in his or her power to become a Producer.

How?

By balancing out the use of the Gap and the Diamond, you balance out *gathering* information and *giving* information when you are with the customer. So you share a greater common ground—and a stronger working relationship.

Of course, most of us have a natural tendency to favor one type of sales activity over the other, depending on our personalities and inclinations. People who are expressive, verbal, and descriptive are more inclined to be *Presenters*. They like to demonstrate and to explain.

Salespeople who are more analytical, on the other hand, tend toward questioning activities. They are more likely to gather data and ask a great number of questions in order to fully analyze and understand a problem.

When you *recognize* your personal style, however, you can modify that style to compensate for your personal tendencies.

For example, I'm a classic Presenter. I *believe* in what I'm selling. I'm also very visual. When I go in to make a sales call, I can't wait to show a film or put on a slide presentation and demonstrate to the prospect everything we have in our program.

I have to *balance* that behavior by making sure I stay in tune with the customer's Operating Reality. I have to remind myself to *stop the process* and say, "Does what I'm saying make *sense* to you? Do you have any *questions* at this point?" Otherwise, I'd be likely to run away with the presentation—and risk leaving the buyer in the dust.

By contrast, I have an associate who's inclined to be an

Interrogator. He's very interested in *all* the information the customer has to give him. So he asks a lot of questions and collects a great deal of information. He has to *balance* his sales call by giving the customer more product and capability data. He has to make sure he brings energy and excitement to his presentation and provides the buyer with enough information so that he is sufficiently convinced to make a decision.

Salespeople who rely on the style of a *Visitor* face the greatest challenge of all.

Some time ago, I was approached near the end of a workshop by a participant who had just filled out a style evaluation sheet for himself. In this confidential evaluation, the participants are asked to reply to a number of questions designed to assess their personal styles of behavior. From the results, each person can tell whether he leans more heavily toward being a Presenter, Interrogator, Visitor, or Producer.

The participant who came up to me was obviously disturbed by what he had learned about himself, and he wanted to share the results of the evaluation with me. But he did not dispute the validity of the test instrument.

"Jack, I think these scores are *right,*" he said.

I asked him to elaborate.

"According to this, I'm a Visitor. And I think that's exactly what I am. I'm making a six-figure salary. I'm bored to tears playing the role of a messenger boy. And I haven't made a serious, new-account sales call in eight years. If I didn't have my boat, the Boston Bruins, and tennis, I'd go nuts."

This, from a salesman *who was making well over a hundred thousand a year!*

He was *successful* by everyone else's standards. But unsuccessful by his own standards, which were: "What am I doing on a day-to-day basis to challenge myself?"

In order to do that, he had to turn himself from a Visitor into a Producer.

. . .

Often, I can tell whether a salesperson is a Presenter, Interrogator, Visitor, or Producer just by observing the language he uses. By "language" I don't mean *just* the words. I mean body language, tone of voice, physical presence, and other signals that indicate whether a salesperson is prepared to take the leadership role in a transaction.

Each of these *behavioral styles* has a different effect on the customer. If you've ever listened to a Presenter going full steam, you've probably thought to yourself, "This person is a great storyteller. And he's certainly on a roll right now. But what's in it for *me?*"

Any buyer who faces an Interrogator is likely to think, "This person is just trying to get me to say, 'Yes.' Every answer I give him will be used against me."

If you come in as a Visitor, the buyer is going to wonder, "What's this person *doing* here? I'm busy, and he's wasting my time. Doesn't he realize that? If he's got something to offer, why doesn't he tell me about it?"

The Producer, on the other hand, establishes his credentials by letting the customer know why he's asking his questions. Then he organizes his presentation so the customer is a *participant* in the solution rather than a *recipient* of information-dumping. In the presence of a Producer, the person in the buyer's seat soon realizes, "This person is working out a solution on my behalf—and *my ideas are part of that solution!*"

The solution may be something that neither you *nor* the buyer could have worked out on your own. Because there's mutual sharing of information and exchange of creative ideas, the end-result is a product of *both* of you *working together.* I call this kind of problem-solving:

SYNERGY.

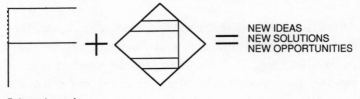

Balanced use of...
GAP *and* DIAMOND *results in* SYNERGY.

That's what happens when a Producer works with a customer.

The point is, you're not just selling a *product.* You're selling *solutions* and *desired outcomes.* So you have to bring your *problem-solving ability* to the relationship.

The leadership role for the relationship is *in your hands.* If you lean toward being a Presenter, balance your behavior with more information-gathering activities. Look to the Gap as a strategy—and before each sales call, ask yourself, "What can I do to increase the common ground? What do I need to *find out* about this person, his organization, and his needs so I can understand his Operating Reality?"

Taken together, the Gap and the Diamond give you a unified *plan* for expanding your position. When you have that plan, you won't be fumbling for words. You don't have to scramble to link your thoughts together. The Gap and the Diamond make the links for you.

That frees you up to be a better listener, because you're not preoccupied with what you're going to do when it's your turn to respond. You are more confident and more *tuned-in.* When you have those models to fall back on, you have a lot of options. There's freedom within a discipline. You're free to become more *creative,* more *expressive,* and more *dynamic.*

As trust, cooperation, and sharing become key elements in

your account relationships, your success with people will achieve a new dimension. When you share common ground, you open the possibility of making your customers your lifelong friends.

11

The Ninth Strategy for Positioning:
Put It in Writing

Long ago, I believed there were *secrets to success* in selling.

So I asked a friend of mine who was a very successful salesman, "Marty, how do you do it? What's your secret?"

"Jack," he said, "it's very simple. Pursue! Pursue! Pursue! You've got to *show up* in the morning, *show up* in the afternoon, *show up* on the weekend."

And that was his advice!

It was good advice, too. Nothing I've learned since would lead me to contradict those words of wisdom.

But today, I would *add something* to what Marty told me back then. My additional advice is this:

PUT IT IN WRITING!

I don't care *what* you're selling, a proposal should go along with it. If you're selling anything that requires a little thought, you need a proposal. Something that involves technology, *you need a proposal.* Anything that has to be installed, implemented, introduced, or inaugurated—YOU NEED A PROPOSAL! It doesn't matter whether you're selling a complex financial planning system, lightning rods, oil wells, insurance, or a fleet of 747s—*use a written proposal!* Above all, if you are a national accounts salesperson, proposal selling is indispensable.

If I were selling my *house* tomorrow, I would write a proposal!

Written proposals have built my company.

They have made fortunes for organizations around the world!

SALESPEOPLE
WHO DON'T WRITE PROPOSALS
ARE MISSING A GOLDEN OPPORTUNITY!

Let's face it, when we think of writing a sales proposal to accompany a contract, document of understanding, or implementation plan, we approach this sales activity with something less than enthusiasm—first, because many of us don't know how to write one; and second, because we don't fully appreciate the power the written word can give us.

The sales proposal written in support of your sales presentation can be a powerful force for:

- Maintaining a presence in front of the buyer
- Selling in your absence
- Eliminating confusion
- Improving secondhand delivery of your recommendations
- Reaching key people you don't have access to

Above all, it serves as a reference point in your efforts to pursue, pursue, pursue. It is the focal point for all of your follow-up activities.

The written proposal contains five sections that back up your verbal presentation in writing. It is the Diamond on paper.

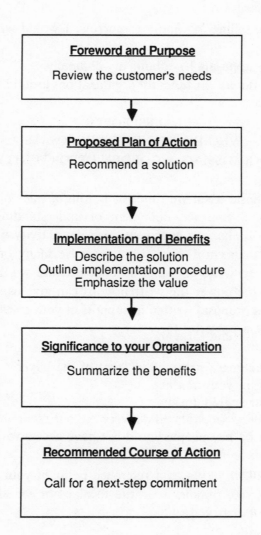

Recently I made a formal two-hour presentation to the presidents of nine divisions of a Fortune 1000 corporation. I knew that even if I made a brilliant presentation, it was unrealistic to expect that *all nine presidents* would lock arms and shout in unison, *"Carew, we like it! We'll take it!"*
Not likely.
After a hard-hitting oral presentation *supported with visuals,* I knew they would ask me the Big Three Questions:

- "What is it going to cost us?"
- "How do we get started?"
- "Where do we go from here?"

I also knew that they would want to discuss the proposal in my absence and reach a decision independent of my presence: this happens in most cases. Knowing this in advance, I prepared a sales proposal entitled:

**Training Proposal
to
The Atlantic Corporation
for
Increased Sales, Profits
and Organizational Excellence**

At the conclusion of the visually supported verbal presentation, I distributed nine copies of the sales proposal, one to each president, for their review and approval.
Included as an addendum to the proposal was a section entitled "Investment Considerations." This independent supplement containing the prices began, "Participation in our program is cost-effective, flexible, and easily managed," then listed the prices, and it concluded, "We fully expect that your in-

creased sales productivity will more than offset the program's cost."

After responding to questions that gave very clear buying signals, I moved into the close.

"Gentlemen, may we begin to increase sales productivity and profits by adopting this proposal today?"

The silence in the room was deafening. I wasn't going to talk anymore. I'd said everything there was to be said.

Suddenly the CEO for the corporation spoke up and said:

> "Jack, thank you for your great presentation, for coming to Miami, and for being with us. However, it's critical that we study the implications and cost considerations of your proposal independent of you. Once this is done and a decision is reached, I will call you with our answer— say, in a week or so."

"Bob," I said, "thank you for your positive response to what I have presented to you today. I understand your desire to want to talk things over as a management team before you make a decision of this significance.

"Now, before we conclude our meeting today, let me be sure I've responded to all of your concerns. Is there anything at all about my company's proposed plan of action that, if not answered today, would prevent you from making a decision to adopt this program?"

Several more questions surfaced, to which I responded.

"Now that we have cleared up these questions, can I work on the assumption that there are no major roadblocks preventing you from discussing the proposal in a positive light and seriously considering its adoption?"

As if by magic, everyone in the room nodded his head in approval or made positive statements like, "It looks good," and "I am excited."

At that moment I made an assumptive statement, "Thank you for your positive responses. I look forward to working along with you in making this program a smashing success."

To keep the momentum going and to make the best investments of time and energy, I went for a concrete next step.

"Bob," I said, "you're a busy man. It's my responsibility to get back to you. May I call you on Tuesday for your decision to implement this program?"

"That will be fine, Jack. Give me a call on Tuesday and I'll have an answer for you."

I did not have to repeat *any* of the proposal, *explain* the next step, or *reiterate* prices—because each of the nine presidents had a copy of *exactly the same proposal* and investment considerations in his hands. And I was confident that after I left and they sat down together, they would all be singing out of the same hymn book.

That meeting was on a Thursday.

On Friday I was back in my Denver headquarters. Within twenty-four hours, letters were sent by *express delivery* to each of the division presidents. By Monday morning, everyone who had heard my presentation and carried away the written proposal now had a letter in front of him saying:

"Thank you for your positive response to the Positional Selling proposal. I feel our program can be a powerful force for increasing sales productivity and organizational excellence within your company. And my organization stands ready to make this happen. May I count on your support to make this a reality?"

On Monday afternoon, I was on the phone to each president. "Did you get my letter? Do you have any further questions? Will you recommend the adoption of this program to Bob?"

On Tuesday, I called Bob. "Now that you've had a chance

to *review the proposal* with your associates, may I, together with you and your nine presidents, begin to increase bottom-line sales results today?"

A proposal . . .

A letter within twenty-four hours . . .

And a telephone call . . .

> *PURSUE!*
>
> *PURSUE!!*
>
> *PURSUE!!!*

The answer was, "Jack, we're going for it. We want to start right away."

Sounds like a fairy tale, doesn't it? Well, I assure you it isn't. This scenario is being repeated a thousand times every day, by sales professionals who have the determination to "go for the gold." Yes, some of them don't always get the order, but enough of us do to make the written proposal an indispensable part of our sales call plan.

The written proposal is the launching pad for all your follow-through *pursuit* activities. What follows are ten ways to maintain and build position.

1. MAKE SURE YOUR PROPOSAL IS SPECIFICALLY DESIGNED FOR THE CUSTOMER

Too many salespeople carry around a pricing sheet or a letter of transmittal, in the form of "We're glad to be with you today, and we feel that . . ." But this kind of "formula package" doesn't do the job.

A real proposal is created expressly *for the individual customer.* It has his name on it! Every word of that document shows that your attention is focused on his exact needs. The plan for implementation and the cost analysis are tailored to fit his organization.

In preparing for your presentation, you may have talked to many people in the organization and asked them questions designed to help you understand the Gap and develop a solution.

Mention these people in your proposal, along with the information they have provided. By doing so, you show the customer that his key players have been instrumental in helping you develop your solution.

2. REFER TO THE PROPOSAL IN YOUR FOLLOW-UP CALLS AND CORRESPONDENCE

If you're dealing with twelve different people in an organization and each of those people has a copy of the same proposal, it becomes a reference point for everyone. They don't need to ask themselves, "Well, what did Bob mean when he said . . . ?" It's right there on paper. That proposal is a *thorough statement of intent.* Everyone is looking at the same data that relates to their decisions. And the document contains answers to their questions:

"How did he say this system worked again . . . ?"

"What were his terms as they related to . . . ?"

THERE'S NO GUESSWORK!

After you leave, those people are going to be studying the plan and considering first steps. You never know what kinds of questions they'll ask. But the proposal has it all! *Refer* to the document:

"Okay, let's go to Section 3 of the proposal. It's in there under Implementation and Benefits."

3. BE READY TO REVISE YOUR PROPOSAL!

Many times, a customer will review your proposal and then say, "I don't think we want this," or "I think we want to try it the other way."

What this means is that you have to go back and modify your proposal. Just respond with the specifics they ask for, then get the proposal back to them immediately.

Recently, I was speaking to the artistic director of an organization that was was seeking corporate sponsorship for a nationwide tour group.

She had just made an extensive proposal to the vice president of public relations of a large corporation, requesting upward of $500,000 in funding.

After Judith had made her presentation, the vice president responded, "I don't think we are ready to make that kind of investment at this time, but I would be glad to recommend a pilot program. I'm having a planning meeting next week. We'll discuss it there."

"Fine," Judith said, "let me get something to you. How many people do you expect at that meeting?"

He told her there would be six.

Judith immediately went back to her office and modified the proposal, replacing it with a two-page summary of a pilot program. She sent six copies to the vice president so he would have one for each of his associates.

When the six decision-makers sat down to talk about sponsorship of the program, *they were all looking at the same thing!* Each of them had a copy of the revised, two-page summary describing the pilot program.

The next day, she had their decision: "We'll go with the pilot!"

"I'm sure revising the proposal made all the difference," Judith told me later. "They didn't have to *guess* what the pilot program would involve. It was all in front of them, summarized in two pages."

4. USE YOUR BEST FRIEND—OVERNIGHT DELIVERY!

I live and die by overnight delivery. Federal Express is *my best friend* because it allows me and my sales team to be in two, three, or four places at the same time.

As soon as I get back to the office, I put together a *pursuit packet* that's picked up the same day.

The next morning, the pursuit packet arrives on the client's desk, and *within the hour,* he has a call from me:

"What's your reaction to the materials I sent you? Do you have any questions? Can we take the next step?"

The pursuit packet may contain only a letter. Or it might include supplemental materials, a further cost-breakdown, or anything else that would interest the client.

Following up the delivery with a phone call helps you *qualify your buyer.* Suppose the package arrives but the client does not answer your call after a sufficient number of tries? You know where you stand with that person—because your "best friend" has helped you find out!

5. SELL ON TWO FRONTS!

I can't emphasize this enough.

You have to sell the customer on your ability to do the job. And then you have to sell the associates in *your own company* on their importance to you in opening up a new account.

That means everything that goes out from your office should be as perfect as you can make it. Letters and documents have to be clean, crisp, neatly folded. No spelling mistakes! If your secretary has a spellchecker on the computer, *use it.* If not, get two people to look over everything that goes out.

Think about how it will look when it arrives. Are documents going to be damaged, bent, and bruised in delivery? Pack them *right,* so they'll arrive as clean as they were when they left your office.

Check the spelling of the name of the company. Check *titles.* Check the names of the people you're dealing with. I tell my secretary: *"Don't trust anything I write down!"* If the person's name and title are not on a document in front of her (a business card, a letter, an annual report), my secretary *calls the company* to make sure the names are spelled correctly and the titles are correct.

If you're sending samples—look at the way they're packaged!

If you're sending documents—look at the binders they're in!

If you're sending letters, cards, or reports—make sure they look the way you want them to look!

Let everyone in your company know that:

SATISFIED CUSTOMERS
ARE THE SUM TOTAL
OF YOUR
ORGANIZATION'S SUCCESS.

Accounts are *won* and accounts are *kept* on the basis of *preparation, execution,* and *follow-through.*

If you're going to *be* the best, you've got to *look the best* and *act like the best!*

6. PUT A TERMINAL POINT ON EVERY TRANSACTION!

There comes a time when the customer says, "Look, Jim, I have all the information. There's no need for you to get back to me. Please, just be patient with me for a few more days and I'll let you know how we did."

"Tom," you say, "you're absolutely right. Thank you for staying on top of this. I know you're busy, and the way I see it, it's my responsibility to get back to you. So let *me* take the responsibility for that, and I'll call you on Wednesday afternoon at two o'clock."

He may say, "No, make it Friday."

And you say, "Fine, Friday at two."

But the point is: You put a *terminal point* on the transaction!

It *is* your responsibility. You're a *salesperson.* You call him. It's not *his* responsibility to call *you!*

7. DON'T GET PUSHED DOWNHILL!

Let's say you've been making calls on the president of the company, and he begins referring you to the second-in-command or other people down the chain of command.

Write to the president! Let him know that you are working with his subordinate and that you'll keep him informed:

Dear Barney,
  As you know, my associates and I are working closely with Jay Crosley. And this is what we're doing . . . And I feel quite certain it will result in . . .
  Thank you for your support. I'll continue to keep you informed . . .

ALWAYS KEEP THE SENIOR-LEVEL
PERSON BRIEFED.

Of course you continue to work with the subordinate. But always keep the senior-level person *fully informed.* This will enable him to support you should you need the weight of his position behind what you are attempting to get done.

8. DON'T GIVE IN TO THE MOOD OF THE BUYER!

If you're not careful, you can catch "Ain't-It-Awfuls" from the buyer. Don't let it happen!

I learned this some time ago when I was following up on a proposal presentation. I knew the buyer well, and we had a good working relationship. But when I got him on the phone the day after the presentation, he began to sing the blues. Things were terrible at the company. He couldn't get to the decision-makers this week. And to top it off, he had some family troubles. Could I just hold on a few days, until things got better?

I made the mistake of feeling sorry for him. I didn't want to push him to the next step. So I found myself backing down.

"Why don't I call you later in the week?" I suggested.

I called him back a few days later and he was out of town. I called back again and he was "out for the afternoon." Again: "He won't be back until next week."

When I finally reached him, he said, "Jack, I'm sorry I didn't get back to you. There have been some changes in the company. I'm afraid we'll have to shelve things for a while. . . ."

The old song.

It was a year and three months later when I finally got the order with that company.

And I realized: I wasn't doing him any favors by feeling sorry for him!

The solution I had would have *helped* him if he had acted on it immediately. My response *should* have been:

> "Bill, I'm concerned about your situation. However there's good news on the horizon! The idea I plan to share with you today will most certainly offset the concerns you've just mentioned to me. Let me explain what I mean."

If someone has serious but unrelated concerns, *acknowledge* the pain that the person may be feeling. Then *position yourself* as someone who's going to be an instrument in taking one aspect of that person's day and turning it into something beneficial.

Don't catch the customer's disease of Ain't-It-Awful. Change that day into a *win* for the customer!

9. CUT THEM OFF AT THE PASS!

When you're making a committee call—a call on a large number of participants—there's always one key decision-maker. You have to get to him *before you leave the room!* So here's what you can do.

At the end of the meeting, wrap it up:

> "Ladies and gentlemen, it was a good meeting. I feel confident that, in working together, we're going to make this a very successful endeavor and a good investment on your part. Thank you."

But as you're leaving the room, *intercept the key person.*

Take the decision-maker aside and ask if you may have a moment with him.

Then look him in the eye. "Terry, if you had to bet next month's rent on whether or not you're going to say 'Yes,' what would you bet?"

And most of the time he'll say, "There are some things we have to talk over, but I'm *sure* we're going to go with it."

"That's good. Count on me to do a great job for you. If anyone has a question, *please* have him talk with me."

What does this do?

It gives you *direct access* to the decision-maker.

It takes decision-making out of the committee—where it's easy to pass along responsibility—and puts it in the hands of an individual. It lets the key person know that you understand the degree of influence he has on the outcome of the pending decision.

And it gives *you* a better idea of *where you stand!*

10. BREAK THE BOUNDARIES!

Believe it or not, you don't have to play "pursuit" by the rules, because *there are no rules!*

You probably won't perform magic tricks in a client's

office—but I told you about the salesperson who did just that
. . . and got away with it!

It's unlikely that you'd set up bowling pins in a doctor's lobby
to get him to come out and talk about medical equipment—yet
I know an outstanding sales professional who not only set up
the game but also awarded prizes to the winner!

You might not make a sales call wearing a tuxedo—but I've
done it once, and I might very well do it again!

When I'm on the road and my secretary is on vacation, I *send
a postcard* to the customer I was with the day before:

> Dear Tom,
>   Great being with you today. As you know,
> I'm on the road. We had a good session, and I
> look forward to working with you.
>
> > In friendship,
> > Jack Carew

My favorite postcard has a picture of the Pope looking upward toward heaven. The message on the card comes right from
the mouth of the Pope: "This program is going to do all the
things Carew said it will. I have it from *my* boss."

It's not a significant thing.

Or is it?

It could even backfire on me.

And has.

It's definitely a risk.

And might not be worth it.

But *you'll never find out what you can do* until you take those
risks—even if it means making mistakes!

Don't just disappear!

Never let go!

Always be in the buyer's consciousness.

Take two minutes *before* and *after* each sales call to break the boundaries and think to yourself: "What is this person's Operating Reality? What will be meaningful to him? What can I do that will make a difference?"

Then *do it!*

Position is not something that comes and goes. *It has to be constant!* You *always* have to be in front of the buyer.

I'm a great believer in *visual impact.* I believe that positive imaging along with putting it in writing helps you sell. Visuals have a positive impact on the people seeing them. They also have an impact on the person using them.

In order to be *in position* with the customer, you have to be a *visible presence.* The written proposal is a visual extension of your verbal presentation. The postcard or letter is a continuation of your conversation. Everything you do to *pursue* makes you a part of the customer's Operating Reality.

SO HE *NEVER* SEES WHAT YOU'RE SELLING
WITHOUT SEEING *YOU!*

And when that happens, you'll never get no for an answer!

12

The Tenth Strategy for Positioning:
Become the Only Choice!

About three years ago, a Positional Selling three-day training workshop was attended by a big-league salesperson who had been a leading producer for twenty years.

Keith Sorensen was a skeptic about Positional Selling.

The decision had been made for him. His company was an aggressive leader in the marketplace, and Keith's boss was intent on improving productivity and profitability.

From Keith's point of view, he didn't *need* to be there. He was doing fine, and he had the sales record to prove it. He was concerned that the program might be another content-free morale booster that would take him away from his sales responsibilities for three days and give him a carload of flashcard techniques that were transparent to every professional buyer in his industry.

As it turned out, Keith was right about one thing.

Management *did* want the sales team to improve. The company was serious about its commitment to sales training.

And I'd promised them, when I sold them the program, that

Positional Selling could *produce* the results they were looking for in their organization.

What Keith's manager *didn't* anticipate—what he couldn't have guessed—was the *change* that took place in Keith Sorensen.

I don't think Keith's manager is quite sure to this day what happened.

"I'd been selling for twenty years and never understood what I was doing," Keith told one of his associates afterward. "I began to realize that the technology of selling can be expressed in simple terms—but it's not a simple business! I discovered that what I'd been doing for twenty years had a *description*. I could finally put a *nameplate* on things I'd been doing all along.

"Positional Selling made me look at selling as a behavioral science. I saw how I could influence change—not only changes in myself, but changes in my customers. This wasn't *theory*. It was *reality*. I had a way to address the needs, values, and motivations of buyers I was seeing every day.

"And when I did that, I improved my batting average. Absolutely!

"By the time I left, I'd undergone a complete change in values and a change in my opinion of myself. I'd looked inside myself and seen something I never had before.

"What Positional Selling has done for my life and my career is immeasurable."

The change that Keith reported was an exaggeration, but not a fabrication.

It was an exaggeration in this sense: The Positional Selling *program* did not bring about the change in Keith's behavior. *Keith* did that! The program just *facilitated* that change by introducing him to the strategies and models of a professional system that has universal meaning for salespeople.

After that, the decision to change was all his.

He used the Positional Selling strategies in the way that they were *designed* to be used—to understand his sales achievements in the past and to improve upon them in the future.

The pride that Keith feels today about his career is entirely the result of the choices he made for himself. It was just fortunate that the Positional Selling strategies were there when he needed them.

With this book I have attempted to make those strategies available to *any salesperson who chooses to use them.*

Already, there are thousands of sales professionals in organizations throughout the world who have energetically embraced the Positional Selling strategies.

Those salespeople share a *language,* a *spirit,* and a set of *common principles* with the highest integrity.

WITHIN ALL OF US IS A CAPACITY FOR GREATNESS

Thirsty people are never satisfied with the status quo. They realize that when you stop getting better, you start getting worse. Decline is inevitable by the mere fact that you do nothing to improve. You constantly have to look for new and different ways to succeed. It's a winner attitude.

I know that's the case because I've seen it shine through in salespeople who have great vision and great values. These people feel an ethical responsibility to operate in the customer's best interest. They have a strong will to win, but that quality is combined with the kindness and respect that wins them people's hearts. They are not self-centered in their relationships with customers, yet they give themselves credit for everything they've got that makes them good.

To achieve greatness you must do things one way—the best way you know how.

LOVE WHAT YOU'RE DOING

If you don't love what you're doing, how can anybody else? Get rid of energy-defeating attitudes about yourself.

Use the energy that is available to you—the energy fueled by your personal beliefs, and also the energy of other people:

Your family.

Your friends.

Your customers.

Selling requires a very human approach to working with people. But it brings you great rewards when you love what you're doing. Value the human skills that you possess and put them to good use on behalf of the people who will be helped by those skills.

Be consistent in the integrity of your commitment. Show your customers that you are dedicated to the profession of selling. You are trying to do the right thing, day in and day out. You will hold fast to the standards you have set for yourself. You will always be in position—a by-product of hard work, thorough precall planning, decisive execution, and diligent pursuit. Demand the best of yourself.

I INVITE YOU TO DO WHAT'S BEST FOR YOU

I ask you to look at where you are today *versus* where you can be in the future. I know that if you energetically embrace the Ten Strategies for Positioning, you will shorten the time it takes to become great.

1. *Take the lead.* You decide how successful you're going to be.

2. *Stop looking out for Number One.* Meeting your needs at the customer's expense does not score points. Operate in the customer's reality and you will be at your professional best. Only when his interests are uppermost in your mind are you at your greatest level of professionalism.

3. *Invest in the relationship.* Have the capacity for warm and rich customer relationships. Don't succumb to "gotcha" tactics that only get you a short-term, one-sided win. If you have patience and use LAER, you and the customer will *both* win.

4. *Bring your energy to the customer.* Use Attitude, Energy, and Appearance to reflect your desire to make Positive Contact with the customer.

5. *Get organized.* Plan each step toward success, and you will lessen the amount of time it takes for you to reach your goals.

6. *Find the area of opportunity.* Dig in and locate what's important to the customer. It's what's important to him that counts.

7. *Make the customer part of the solution.* If you do, the customer will make a commitment to what he helped create.

8. *Assume the responsibility.* Be flexible in your approach to managing the relationship. Its success is your responsibility.

9. *Put it in writing.* Pursue, pursue, pursue! Never give up!

10. *Become the only choice.* Work on your vision of greatness. And go after it now.

YOU DECIDE HOW SUCCESSFUL YOU WILL BE

In the long run, your character will win—even if you stumble along the way.

To fall is not to fail. If you made a bad call, don't let it throw